A GROWTH MINDSET

WORKBOOK FOR TEENS

A Practical 8-Week Guide to Cultivate Resilience, Solve Problems, and Ignite Confidence Using Clinically Crafted Activities for Real Life

JILL BROMLEY, LPC

LICENSED THERAPIST

Copyright©2025 Jill Bromley

All rights reserved.

No portion of this book may be reproduced in any form without written permission from the publisher or author, except as permitted by U.S. copyright law.

ISBN: 979-8-218-57939-5 Paperback

CONTENTS

A Letter to Parents: Why This Workbook Matters   1

Introduction What is this Approach About?   7

Week One: Growth Mindset and the Mind-Brain Connection   11

    What is a Growth Mindset?   11

    What is The Mind-Brain Connection?   14

    Journal Activity   16

    What Is the Thinking Mind, and How Does It Work?   17

    How Thoughts Create Experiences   19

    Journal Activity   22

    What are Negative Thought Programs?   23

    Important Point: Mission-Critical   24

    What are Neural Networks, and What Is Neuroplasticity?   25

    Important Point- The Process is the Same   30

    Focus of the Week   30

Week Two: Intention and Awareness   33

    Intention   33

    Common Excuses   34

    Awareness   38

    Important Point: Reactions   39

    Journal Activity   40

Focus of the Week	41
Week Three: Identification	**43**
Important Point: Fear	46
Important Point: Counterintuitive Logic	49
Journal Activiy	50
Technique: Running a Mind Diagnostic	51
Important Point: Defensive Firewalls	52
Technique: Interview with the Negative	53
Journal Activity	58
Focus of the Week	**59**
Week Four: Rejection and Separation	**61**
Rejection	61
Technique: Rejection	61
Separation	62
A Note About Coping	64
Technique: Separation	66
Technique: Visualize The Negative	66
Drawing Activity	68
Technique: Dealing with Trauma-Based Reactions	69
Cognitive Behavior Therapy (CBT)	70
Technique: Thought Challenging	71
Technique: Thought Reframing/Neutralizing	71
Important Point: Disengage From the Negative	72
Journal Activity	74

    Focus of the Week   75

Week Five: Focal Points   77

    Technique: Mantras and Affirmations   78

    Journal Activity   81

    Important Point: External vs Internal   82

    Technique: Narrative and Visualization   82

    Important Point: Large vs Small Events   82

    Journal Activity   85

    Important Point: The Power of Visualization   86

    Drawing Activity   88

    Technique: Sleep-Wake Routine   89

    Important Point: Expect Positive Experiences   89

    Focus of the Week   91

Week Six: Shifting   93

    Technique: Shifting with Memory and Attention   94

    Time Frames   96

    Important Point: Neutrality   98

    Journal Activity   100

    Emotions and Energy   101

    Technique: Deal with Negative Emotions   103

    Journal Activity   105

    Focus of the Week   106

Week Seven: States and Aligned Experiences   **107**

What is a State?	107
Important Point: Thoughts vs. States	108
States Self-Perpetuate	109
Short-Term Effects	112
Long-Term Effects	112
Manifestations in Professional Practice	113
Important Point: "Dis-ease"	114
Focus of the Week	115
Week Eight: Anchoring	**117**
Internal Anchoring	117
External Anchoring	117
Exposures	118
Media	118
Important Point: Making Behavioral Changes	120
Other people	121
Journal Activity	123
Actions	124
Journal Activity	126
Important Point: Mind-Brain and Body Harmony	127
Clearing Persistently Negative Thought Programs	128
Technique: Breathwork	128
Technique: The Emotional Freedom Technique (EFT)	128
Focus of the Week	**131**

Wrap-Up: Conclusion and Tips For Success   **133**

   Conclusion   **133**

   14 Tips for Success   **137**

References   **141**

Appendix   **147**

   Part One: Internal Anchoring Techniques   **148**

   Part Two: External Anchoring Techniques:
      Mind your Exposures and Do the Do's!   **151**

   Part Three: Bonus Activity: The Rice Experiment   **169**

   Anchoring Techniques Conclusion:
      Be Intentional, Own Your Life   **172**

A Letter to Parents: Why This Workbook Matters

As a licensed therapist with over two decades of experience in behavioral health and clinical education, I have witnessed a critical gap in how we approach mental health and personal development for our children. This workbook is more than just another self-help guide—it is a transformative approach to understanding how our minds truly work. I have distilled decades of clinical experience into an accessible, science-backed approach that actually works. Gain all the benefits of professional mental wellness expertise for your child without the time commitment and expense of traditional therapy.

The Power of a Growth Mindset:

In a world that often feels overwhelming, a growth mindset is not just beneficial—it is essential. It is the difference between a child who sees challenges as insurmountable obstacles and one who views them as opportunities for learning and growth.

What makes this approach unique is its focus on the mind-brain connection. We are not just teaching coping mechanisms or surface-level strategies. We are providing a deep, scientifically grounded understanding of how thoughts shape brain function, emotions, and behaviors.

Why This Matters Now More Than Ever:

• Mental health challenges are increasing among teens.

• Traditional approaches often fall short of providing real, lasting tools.

• Young people need more than just symptom management—they need empowerment.

• Teenage brains have incredible neuroplasticity, making this the perfect time to develop resilience.

What Sets This Workbook Apart:

1. Science-Backed Methodology

This approach synthesizes the most effective elements from evidence-based practices—drawing on Cognitive Behavioral Therapy (CBT), mindfulness, and solution-focused therapies and grounding them in our latest understanding of brain functioning, particularly neuroplasticity. We are moving beyond traditional therapeutic techniques that merely process emotions. Instead, we are equipping teens with the ability to actively shape their experiences by understanding the profound, intricate relationship between mind and brain.

2. Narrative-Based Learning

Forget rigid lesson plans and dry educational content. This workbook speaks directly to teens in their language, avoiding clinical jargon while never "talking down" to them. The content flows naturally, building from one concept to the next in an engaging, conversational style.

3. Comprehensive and Inclusive

This workbook is designed primarily for teens, but its principles are universal and transformative. The techniques and insights within transcend diagnostic categories—regardless of whether a teen has no clinical diagnosis, one diagnosis, or multiple diagnoses. These tools are relevant for all, ensuring no one feels excluded.

Even younger children can benefit from the techniques with parental guidance, and adults will find equally powerful insights. Mental growth isn't about a label—it is about understanding how our minds work and learning to harness our potential.

A Note on Vocabulary and Learning:

You will notice intentionally introduced vocabulary words. This is not about complexity—it is about expanding understanding. Learning new words is a powerful tool for cognitive development at any age.

A Note on Medication:

This approach is not a replacement for medication, nor do I advocate for people to be on medication or not to be on medication. Those are personal decisions between a patient and a medical doctor. Medication has its place; however, it cannot and does not change how a person thinks or address the true nature of thoughts. It cannot provide new thought patterns or be responsible for shaping new positive life experiences. Medication can help control symptoms so that people can make the best use of therapeutic approaches like this.

My Motivation:

Over years of clinical practice, I have heard countless adults say, "I wish I knew this when I was younger," or "I wish they taught us this stuff when we were kids!" This workbook is my answer to that wish. It is an opportunity to equip the next generation with tools for mental resilience, self-understanding, and personal growth. I intend for it to be more than just a guide. It is a toolkit for thriving.

How to Use This Workbook:

- Go through it together as a family.
- Create a supportive, open environment.
- Practice the techniques collectively.
- Empower and support each other's growth journeys.

Our Collective Responsibility:

As parents and caregivers, we are crucial in teaching our children how to develop and maintain healthy minds. In a world of increasing complexity and challenge, these skills are not just helpful—they are vital.

I sincerely hope that this content will prompt the participation of parents and other trusted adults to hold productive conversations with their kids. Kids do not exist in a vacuum—

they exist within the context of family units and can make substantial progress when their collective supports them. Guide your child on their journey of understanding, growth, and empowerment with your steadfast support.

Introduction
What is this Approach About?

Imagine if you had a user manual for your brain. Not some boring textbook that puts you to sleep, but a real guide that helps you understand how your mind actually works. A way to hack your own potential, turn challenges into opportunities, and become the most authentic version of yourself.

This is that manual. And it is going to teach you something powerful: how to develop a growth mindset.

Over the past two decades, I have worked with countless people - teens, adults, people struggling with everything from anxiety to career challenges - and here is what I have learned: Your thoughts are not just random brain noise. They are the software that runs your entire life experience. How you think literally shapes your brain, your emotions, your behaviors, and your outcomes.

This workbook is your roadmap to developing a growth mindset. It is not about fixing something that is "broken." It is about upgrading your internal operating system and building infrastructure that works for you- not against you.

We are going to do something revolutionary. We will explore what I call the **mind-brain connection** - how your thoughts interact with your physical brain to create your lived experience. You will learn why your teenage brain is uniquely positioned to develop incredible mental flexibility. Neuroplasticity is not just a scientific term - it is your superpower.

What you will find inside is not just another self-help book. It is a personalized journey - an 8-week roadmap to understanding yourself, building genuine confidence, and developing the kind of resilience that will serve you for life.

Why is a growth mindset so important? Because it:

- Turns obstacles into opportunities.
- Builds real, lasting confidence.
- Helps you bounce back from setbacks.
- Prepares you for real-world challenges.
- Gives you control over your own personal development.

You will get:

- Essential concepts and definitions
- 8 transformative weeks to developing a growth mindset
- 14 journaling prompts that will make you think
- 14 success tips that cut through the noise
- 33 bonus anchoring techniques to keep leveling up your mind

WHAT IS THIS APPROACH ABOUT?

Whether you are dealing with school stress, social challenges, performance anxiety, or just want to understand yourself better, this workbook is your toolkit. And the best part? This approach benefits EVERY teen, even if you're dealing with anxiety, depression, neurodivergence, trauma, learning struggles, or simply the everyday turmoil of being a teen. This is for anyone who wants to unlock their potential.

Ready to become the architect of your own experience?

Let us dive in.

Week One

Growth Mindset and the Mind-Brain Connection

What is a Growth Mindset?

A growth mindset means viewing yourself and your life as something you can enhance and continually develop through learning, effort, and perseverance. Difficulties and setbacks become opportunities instead of personal failures or dead-ends. Viewing disappointments in a neutral way instead of internalizing that something is inherently wrong with you is critical- like data points on a spreadsheet...it is just information. You begin to value feedback instead of fearing judgment. The success of others inspires you, and you realize that you, too, can achieve and grow. You embrace challenges and the efforts necessary for learning and then seek more ways to expand.

Take, for example, a situation where you may have been disappointed or, even worse, crushed by perceived failure. Maybe you wanted to gain entrance into a particular program or sports team. But you were rejected. This situation eventually happens to everyone at some point in their lives. And if you are a particularly ambitious person, it will happen to you more than once- simply because ambition requires pursuits. Now, while you are warranted in feeling down about a situation such as this- having strong, negative emotional reactions (falling to pieces) and conclusive thoughts (you are a failure and nothing works out for you) limits your ability to succeed in this situation and those that follow. This is what is commonly known as a "fixed mindset."

However, if you acknowledged the disappointment as a normal feeling that anyone would have, gave yourself a chance to feel and process it, and refused to engage in self-defeating or victimized thinking, you would have cleared the way for your next pursuit. If you adopted a perspective that this experience was just data, which in and of itself had no greater implications about your self-worth or value, and instead saw it as valuable and necessary information to steer your next move, well, this is called a growth mindset.

You do not know what is in the cards for you. None of us do for certain. We must trust that our experiences are meant to guide us in the right direction, so long as we can look at things objectively, without the distorted lens of emotional reactivity and limiting beliefs. Often, when a door gets slammed in our face, it just means, "That's not the right door; there is a much better door over there; please redirect." Imagine if you heard that voice every time a perceived setback occurred - I am certain you would stand tall, smile, and say, "Thanks!"

I can say with absolute certainty that no one who ever achieved greatness, be it small personal triumphs or monumental successes that impacted societies, possessed fixed mindsets. This is actually a topic of study, such that many books have been written about the qualities of highly successful people. Guess what we know? Luck, fortune, demographics, or other external factors were not responsible for their successes. In fact, they seemed able to conjure these factors with their mindsets and corresponding successes. Hmmmm. Just let that percolate for now...

Ok- so, achieving a growth mindset requires developing a positive way of perceiving yourself and your role in your life.

It requires developing new patterns of thinking and behaving. But this is easier said than done and certainly no small feat! How does one go about making these kinds of changes? What will enable you to acquire these skills? Why- learning about the mind-brain connection, of course!

What is The Mind-Brain Connection?

The mind-brain connection describes the relationship between the thinking mind and the physical brain and ultimately explains why we have the life experiences we do. It reveals why and how we possess certain thinking, feeling, and behavior patterns. It explains our perceptions and why we can get stuck in negative mindsets and have recurring negative experiences.

The mind-brain connection approach has many benefits. Not only does it lead to a growth mindset, but it also teaches how to take control of one's mind and shape the experiences you want to have. You will expand your awareness of yourself by unlocking the mysteries of the human mind and the physical brain. You will better understand how some people seem to draw positive outcomes to themselves, and you will be able to achieve that, too.

To accomplish this, I must first introduce you to a few fundamental concepts about the mind-brain connection. But before we get into the nitty-gritty, let us first identify what YOU want to get out of this!

What do you want to get out of your journey toward a growth mindset? Be intentional and write a list below. Consider areas of your life such as school, sports/activities, socialization, family, or mental health.

What Is the Thinking Mind, and How Does It Work?

No one doubts that we think. Yet, we cannot see or touch a thought. Ancient philosophers (deep thinkers) have used thinking as evidence to prove that we exist. "I think therefore I am," was declared by Renee Descartes around the mid-1600s. "The energy of the mind is the essence of life," was stated by Aristotle around the mid-300s B.C. While this workbook is not meant to delve into philosophical reasoning, it bears mentioning because the topic of thinking has been on the minds of humans for eons! I have yet to encounter a person or a text disputing that we think or that thinking is unrelated to the very nature of our existence!

Thoughts are the product of the invisible mind. The physical brain and our life experiences influence them but are not the ultimate authority on their contents. Most people do not understand this, believing that their brain is the source of thought, that it is a fixed system, and that, as a result, it is outside of their control.

The mind and brain are interconnected, constantly feeding information back and forth. This relationship is what I call the mind-brain connection. The mind is very powerful- it can influence and change the brain in profound ways, though unfortunately, most of us experience the brain influencing and changing the mind.

Physical experiences such as pain or suffering are very powerful influencers of the mind. Imagine something very negative, like witnessing or experiencing violence. These physical experiences will cause the brain to send information to the mind, generating thinking consistent with that experience and shaping the person's perceptions of the world. Perhaps the thinking becomes about avoiding certain places or people, or worse, about self-judgment related to what happened.

When the brain and physical experiences become the dominant influencers of the thinking mind, we tend to have more negative experiences and often find ourselves in negative patterns or loops. This is because we allow ourselves to focus on what is external to us to dictate our thinking instead of using the sheer might of the internal thinking mind to influence our external experiences. With the mind-brain approach, we seek to ensure that our thinking flows in the proper direction, free from as much "backwash" interference as possible!

Now, I need to make a note about terminology regarding the mind. You may have heard of the conscious and unconscious/subconscious mind. These terms subdivide the mind into two aspects: one that we have awareness of (conscious) and one that we are unaware of (subconscious). This topic can get pretty complicated and a bit tangential to the material we will cover, but just know that sometimes we are aware of our thoughts (conscious), and sometimes we are not (subconscious). The goal is always to increase awareness of the contents of the subconscious mind so that we have a better understanding of the thoughts that influence us. This makes them conscious. It is a necessary life-long process and often a focal point of therapeutic work because developing awareness of the subconscious mind can lead to profound life transformations. I frequently describe this to people as being able to move information from the "back to the front" of the mind. You will learn how to do this in Week Three.

For simplicity, I will use one term, "the mind," from here on out. When I talk about increasing awareness of the contents of the mind, I am referring to the process described above.

How Thoughts Create Experiences

It is important to know that our thinking, emotions, and behaviors are congruent, which means that they reflect or match one another. For example, if you have anxious or nervous thoughts, you will also feel anxious, nervous, apprehensive, stressed, or the like. Furthermore, your behavior will also match or reflect these thoughts and emotions.

Behaviors are highly specific to each person. To build insight and awareness, you must become aware of the types of behaviors that you engage in when experiencing a negative emotion, such as anxiety. For example, some people cry, pace, hide, avoid things, or even become confrontational! Regardless of your individualized behaviors, know they will always coincide with your thoughts and emotions.

Due to congruency, we can discover the nature of our thinking by identifying our emotional state or behaviors and vice versa. This trick can be used if you are unsure about the nature of your thoughts, which is actually a common experience!

Let me elaborate on congruency and why we focus on thinking to improve control over our emotions and behaviors (experiences) with this metaphor:

Imagine a train. The engine represents our thoughts/thinking, the cars represent our emotions/feelings, and the caboose represents our behaviors/actions. Now, if you wanted to change something about this train- its speed, its direction, or maybe you want it on a different track altogether, would you focus your efforts and attention on changing something about the middle or the end of the train? No, you would not. It might have some effect, but it certainly would not be as effective as focusing on the engine. When we change something about the engine, the rest of the train follows because it is attached and has to follow. This is very similar to how our thoughts, feelings, and behaviors work. As stated above, feelings and behaviors (experiences) follow along with our thinking because of congruency.

WEEK ONE

Think of a time when you were unsure of either what your thoughts were, how you were feeling, or even how you were acting (sometimes this happens)! What would the third naturally be if you could identify two of them? Follow the rules of congruency. This is a useful exercise to visualize how thoughts, emotions, and behaviors are connected. Can you see how your thinking created the way you felt and acted?

WEEK ONE

What are Negative Thought Programs?

Thought programs are established patterns of thinking within the mind, typically in the part we are unaware of (subconscious), but not always. Sometimes, we are overwhelmed by our thought programs, such as when we can consciously "hear" them going on and on about things to worry about or be afraid of.

Unfortunately, most of us have quite a bit of negativity ingrained into our thought patterns, which, due to the concept of congruency, causes us to experience unwanted things like anger, sadness, loneliness, and fear. This ingrained negative thinking is what I call "negative thought programs." So- the negative thought programs cause our bad feelings and behaviors.

Negative thought programs cause us to feel bad

Most people develop counterproductive, negative thinking and never question it. Adults grow up and say things like, "That's just the way I am," or "That's just the way my mind works" or "It's genetic," or "It's brain chemistry," insinuating that nothing can be done. That is just plain wrong and commonly known as limiting beliefs or limiting belief systems.

Interestingly enough, limiting beliefs are hallmarks of fixed mindsets—they literally keep us "limited" and "fixed" in counterproductive patterns. Since we are going for growth mindsets, rooting out and changing this type of thinking and believing is "mission-critical!"

Important Point: Mission-Critical

You will encounter the term "mission-critical" again throughout the book. Whenever you see it, know that I am underscoring the importance of the concept or technique toward achieving a growth mindset with the mind-brain approach.

Neuroscience has advanced quite a bit over the last decades, and we now know that the mind-brain is basically programmed and programmable—not too much different from a computer (Hanson, 2013; Lipton, 2015). What do we do when something is wrong with our computer's programming? We fix it before it causes more problems! That is exactly what we will do with our own thought programs. But first, we have to know what they are.

It takes some good detective work to discover the types of thought patterns within the mind because, as I stated earlier, many are outside our immediate awareness. We want to become skilled detectives because this helps us discover what influences our thoughts, feelings, and behaviors and because...wait for it...this is a major concept... these patterns actually form neural networks in our brains!

Yes, our habitual patterns of thinking can alter our physical brain. Let that sink in for a moment... because it implies quite a lot about how we feel, act, and generally experience our lives.

What are Neural Networks, and What Is Neuroplasticity?

I promise to do my best not to make this section long and boring- but I do have to explain some things! This is not intended to be a lesson in neuropsychology, so I will provide an overview and list various references and resources at the end of the workbook if you want to research this topic further. In fact, if you simply looked up the topic of "neuroplasticity" or the term "rewire your brain," you will find volumes of books written by doctors, scientists, therapists, personal growth experts, spiritual leaders, etc. It is not difficult to find reading material on this subject!

As I introduced above, the brain is much like a computer—an unbelievable processor of complex information that we still do not fully understand. Perhaps you have heard this before? This comparison is becoming increasingly common, and I encounter it frequently.

This means that, like a computer, the brain is programmable. Neuroscientists have been studying this for a long time and found that the brain develops networks that automatically run without our conscious awareness due to the information fed to it by our thinking. That makes things efficient in the sense that we do not have to pay attention to our thoughts all the time; they are just running in the background, dictating how we think, feel, and act in all different circumstances. Pretty convenient- unless those networks are not helpful!

Neural networks are the connections among neurons found in the brain. Some of these connections involve small amounts of neurons, while others are massive! Nothing exists in isolation in the sense that these networks link or connect all over the brain in very complex ways. Our brain is filled with them, and they are responsible for how our brain functions! Our brain is very active, connecting new neurons to create neural networks all of the time, especially when it is engaged in new learning, having new experiences, or intentionally focused on a particular topic (Robinson, 2024).

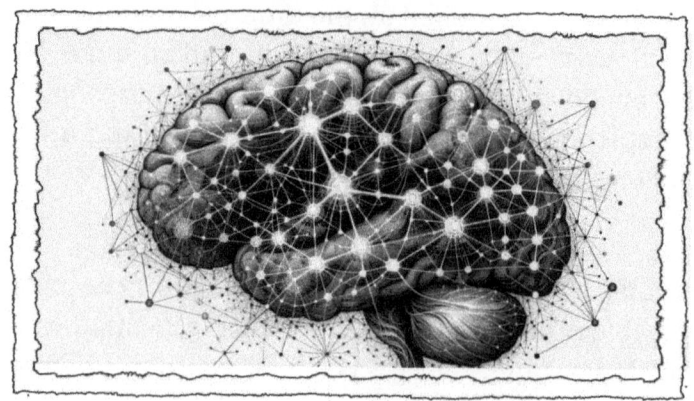

This means you can influence these physical brain structures with intentional acts! Intentional focus is a mission-critical concept I will discuss in greater detail in Week Five. It is truly amazing to discover that we can actually change some aspects of our neurological functioning. This is known as neuroplasticity (Simpkins & Simpkins, 2012).

Neuroplasticity refers to the concept that the brain is "plastic" or can change and even "rewire." Here is one definition provided by a Google search: "The ability of the brain to form and reorganize synaptic connections, especially in response to learning or experience or following injury." Another definition, provided by Wikipedia, states: "Neuroplasticity, also known as neural plasticity or brain plasticity, is the ability of neural networks in the brain to change through growth and reorganization. It is when the brain is rewired to function in some way that differs from how it previously functioned. These changes range from individual neuron pathways making new connections to systematic adjustments like cortical remapping or neural oscillation...Neuroplasticity was once thought by neuroscientists to manifest only during childhood, but research in the latter half of the 20th century showed that many aspects of the brain can be altered (or are "plastic") even through adulthood. However, the developing brain exhibits a higher degree of plasticity than the adult brain."

To be clear, I am definitely not basing this book on Google or Wikipedia searches! However, I wanted to provide two of the most straightforward and mainstream accepted definitions so you understand these concepts are not out of left field! Generations ago, scientists believed that the brain was fixed and unable to make new neural pathways or change itself.

However, now we know that this is totally untrue!

Consider reading or listening to Norman Doidge's (2007) book The Brain That Changes Itself: Stories of Personal Triumph from the Frontiers of Brain Science. This New York Times bestseller catalogs many fascinating and incredible stories of people with all kinds of conditions, including physical disabilities, who were able to change their physical brains due to neuroplasticity. It's totally worth the read!

Finally, we know that the degree of plasticity, or the brain's ability to change, comes easiest at younger ages and depends upon our intentions, ability to focus on those intentions, and consistency of our actions. Again, young people have the advantage here (Sweeton, 2017)! Notice the concept of intentional focus coming up again?

As I mentioned earlier when explaining thought programs, it is very common, and almost a condition of being human, that we get stuck with a lot of negative thoughts. Some are small and not too controlling yet still influence us, while some are big, influence us a lot, and are very controlling. But we can still deal with them. The good news is that even if we change the smaller, less controlling programs, we are taking power and influence away from the bigger, more controlling ones (Sweeton, 2017).

As previously mentioned and bears repeating, the brain forms new neural networks all the time, every day (Hanson, 2013). However, unless you make these networks stick to become what I call "hardwired," they will not take hold enough to create new patterns of thoughts, feelings, or behaviors.

WEEK ONE

Therefore, not only is it our job to become fully aware of the already hardwired negative thought programs, but it is also our responsibility to do what we need to do so that we can create new hardwiring. Otherwise, we are stuck using a thinking network that does not serve us- and we know that this will cause us to have feelings and behaviors that are consistent with that network!

So- if we are tired of having the same old experiences but keep relying on the same old patterns of thinking, feeling, and acting to solve our problems, well– nothing much will change. How can it? Think about the train metaphor from earlier- that "train of thought" or "brain train" will just keep rolling down the same fixed set of tracks, winding up at the same station, and providing you with the same outcomes because that is what it is designed to do! Therefore, we must do something to change its route or its line.

Same old outcomes unless you change the looping train of thought

Important Point: The Process is the Same

The process of creating thought patterns and neural networks works the same for both negative and positive types of thought programs. If you ever get confused along the way, you can always look at how the negative functions and reverse engineer! Also, you can shorten the time this process takes by sticking to your intentions, honing your focus, and being consistent.

Focus of the Week:

Our first chapter introduced many new concepts and definitions that may seem overwhelming! Specifically, I defined the foundational concepts of a growth mindset and how using the mind-brain connection approach will help you attain it! Then, I delved into descriptions of the thinking mind, how thoughts create experiences (congruency), negative thought programs, neural networks, and neuroplasticity.

The takeaway is that our brains are programmable, like computers. Through intentional focus and consistent effort, we can create new neural pathways that support a growth mindset, replacing limiting beliefs and negative thought patterns that keep us stuck in fixed mindsets.

I provided two journaling exercises to complete before Week Two. These are not meant to be burdensome homework assignments! I simply want this content to be personalized and meaningful for you. The more you connect with these concepts, the more value you will get from the effort you have put forth!

Week Two

Intention and Awareness

Intention

Setting a clear intention is simple: make a conscious choice about what you want and have the will to pursue it. That is all. Ask yourself: Do you truly intend to learn these concepts? Do you intend to apply them to improve your life? Be decisive. Vague or halfhearted intentions will not serve you – that is the trap people fall into when they doubt change is possible or fear failure. Personal mastery comes through practice, and that is absolutely within your power.

You might think it is trivial that setting an intention is crucial for success. But it is absolutely true. Without clear intentions, everything else falters – including your results! Throughout my years of work, I have seen countless people who claimed they wanted to feel better but never truly committed to that intention. Invariably, they progressed far more slowly than those who were intentional about their goals.

Perhaps you believe that having a diagnosis or disability prevents you from setting and pursuing clear intentions. Nothing could be further from the truth! I know this to be true because I spent my career working with people diagnosed with all sorts of conditions. I will explore this more deeply in Weeks Three and Seven, but I have heard every variation of this concern. Let me share some common examples before your negative mind-brain starts spinning any questionable stories...

Common Excuses

"But I have ADHD, and I cannot focus. I cannot pay attention long enough to follow through."

Let me show you why this thinking is flawed: intense focus and high productivity are actually ADHD symptoms! Anyone familiar with ADHD knows that people with this condition can focus on topics of their interest far longer than those without it. It is practically a superpower in the right situations. The key is that the subject matter needs to be stimulating and engaging to that person. So, if you decide this material is truly important to you, you can focus on it with equal or greater intensity than anyone else.

"But I have depression and can't be happy! It prevents me from accomplishing anything."

Depression is actually concentrated attention on everything negative. Your brain delivers on these thoughts, leading to unhappiness, defeatism, and low energy. People with depression have remarkable powers of focus – they are just directed at the negative. The more you ruminate, the deeper the depression. Imagine if that level of intense focus and rumination were to be intentionally directed toward a different type of thinking.

"But I have anxiety. I am fearful and worried all the time. I even have paralyzing attacks."

Anxiety and fear grow through our deliberate focus on potential threats – real or imagined. We strengthen these fear-based neural pathways by constantly directing attention to past struggles, imagined catastrophes, and future worries. But here is the key: this same mechanism reveals your power to choose differently. Through intention, you can redirect your focus away from the spiral of "what-ifs."

"But I have OCD. My thoughts are intrusive and stressful, and I cannot control them. I am compelled to perform certain rituals to feel relief."

The very nature of OCD – the intense focus on thoughts and rituals – are the elements required to form strong neural pathways. When you repeatedly connect thoughts with specific behaviors, you strengthen these brain connections. Here is the empowering truth: intentional, focused practice of new thought patterns can weaken these OCD circuits by creating new, positive ones. You already possess the neuroplasticity to reprogram your mind – it is simply about consciously directing it toward healthier pathways.

"But I have trauma that has hardwired my brain to be in the mode of fear and reactivity at the drop of a hat."

Trauma reactions occur when past events intrude into the present through neural pathways activated by triggers. These pathways can flood you with distressing thoughts and feelings, pulling your focus away from the present moment. But you have more power than you might realize! Through intentional awareness, you can learn to recognize these reactions as echoes of the past rather than current threats.

When trauma reactions arise, you can ground yourself in the present with intentional practices. This will gradually build new neural pathways supporting your healing while weakening the old trauma-created pathways.

"But I'm autistic. I have difficulty understanding others, communicating well, and being flexible."

While autism shapes how you experience the world, your ability to focus intensely on topics of interest is actually a powerful strength you can intentionally direct. Your natural capacity for deep focus and detailed attention can be channeled toward mastering new skills, including social communication and flexibility. Autism does not determine which topics you choose to explore deeply – that intentional choice belongs to you.

"But I just can't! I have tried!"

As Yoda said: "Do or do not. There is no try." I do not care that Yoda was a movie character – he was 100% correct. Success comes in all sizes: tiny victories, complete transformations, and everything in between. Even the smallest successes come from being intentional and "doing." "Trying" is just a preemptive excuse to avoid accountability and expect failure. "I tried" is almost always followed by "and I can't" or "and it didn't work." In other words, "I'm going to fail, so why bother with the effort?" Do the effort! "Do the do's" is my Yoda-like phrase, though clearly not as famous!

"But I don't know how!"

Even when given direct instruction, some people insist they do not know how to do anything. This represents mental energy focused solely on defeatism rather than on anything positive or productive. It is a setup for failure that creates a no-win situation every time.

Okay, I think I have established that the negative mind commonly resists when faced with the brass tacks of intentional change. Norman Doidge, M.D., in his book, The Brain That Changes Itself (2007), explains this when he stated, "While the human brain has apparently underestimated itself, neuroplasticity isn't all good news; it renders our brains not only more resourceful but also more vulnerable to outside influences. Neuroplasticity has the power to produce more flexible but also more rigid behaviors– a phenomenon I call the "plastic paradox." Ironically, some of our most stubborn habits and disorders are products of our plasticity" (Preface location 144).

With Doidge's research, we understand that the process of creating thought programs and neural networks works in both directions and that it is 100% possible to conquer the toughest of symptoms because we never lose brain plasticity. So, while it may be true that having a clinically diagnosed condition can make it difficult to perform similarly to non-disabled peers in some areas, it does NOT mean that you cannot improve, progress, and achieve in areas that will significantly improve your functioning. Never align yourself with being disabled. You are not a disability; you are a whole and complete person who functions in your own unique ways with your own neuroplasticity, just like everyone else!

Awareness

After setting intentions, the next step is to recognize when negative thought programs are active. We must become aware—mindfully aware! Increasing awareness of what is happening in our minds is another mission-critical factor.

Negative thought programs tend to become active due to a trigger, which I define as a situation, event, or circumstance that causes the negative thought program to become activated, come "online," or become the most dominant and controlling thought you are experiencing. A trigger can be almost anything: something someone says or does, something you see or hear, somewhere you go, or something that happens around you.

Sometimes, we notice negative thought programs aside from when a noticeable trigger happens, such as during downtimes when we are not busy, like when we are trying to fall asleep, when we wake up in the middle of the night, or when trying to read or do homework. When we are not distracting ourselves with busy activities, these thoughts can be experienced more consciously. And then they can get really bothersome because they interfere with our ability to be productive or rest.

Other indications that a negative thought program is active are cues like becoming emotionally or physically reactive, experiencing physical reactions like hot hands, teeth/fist clenching, breathing fast, muscle tightness, restlessness, sudden fatigue, sudden pain/sickness, or sometimes even "hearing" your negative thoughts because they are so intrusive!

Important Point: Reactions

Big reactions, those that really get the best of you, or sudden physical ailments from out of nowhere are frequently due to a negative thought program coming online!

Practice your awareness! When are you aware that a negative thought program has become active? What are some triggers that you experience?

Focus of the Week:

For week two, I explored two foundational concepts: intention and awareness. I explained that setting clear intentions is not just about wanting change but about making a conscious choice and having the will to pursue it. I also addressed common excuses people make about why they cannot change, showing how these very "limitations" often reveal hidden strengths.

I emphasized that diagnoses and disabilities do not prevent you from setting and pursuing clear intentions. In fact, many conditions like ADHD, depression, anxiety, and OCD demonstrate your powerful ability to focus and create strong neural pathways - it is just about redirecting that power positively.

Finally, I explained how to develop awareness of negative thought programs by recognizing triggers and physical reactions. I would like you to practice setting your intentions and being mindfully aware. Do not forget to write them in your journal prompts (see Week One's prompt for "What do you want to get out of your journey toward a growth mindset?" to help you with your intentions). It might seem simple, but you will have missed a foundational skill for successfully attaining a growth mindset without practicing intention and recognizing when negative thought programs are active.

Awareness is a discipline of intentional self-observation and nothing to sneeze at. Have you ever heard of Tibetan Buddhist monks? They famously live in solitude from modern society to practice techniques that develop mindfulness and expanded awareness. Their abilities are renowned and have been the focus of many studies. Now, I am not asking you to become a Tibetan Buddhist monk; I am just pointing out that awareness is such a significant topic that an entire society devotes itself to it!

Week Three

Identification

This week, we will build on your powers of intention and awareness by learning about and identifying specific negative thought programs running in your mind. If you recall from Week One, sometimes we are aware of them because they are in our conscious mind, and other times we are not because they are in our subconscious mind, beyond our immediate awareness. Oftentimes, they move from the background to the forefront after a triggering event, which is a great time to detect them. Other times, they become bothersome when we are trying to be still or productive at studying.

Let me first address some sources of negative thought programs known to influence us:

- Our genetics/biology can predispose us to over/underactivity in certain brain regions.
- Our development and the conditions under which we are raised, especially during the critical and sensitive periods of development (Hensch, 2015).
- The adoption of belief systems taught to us by our family.
- Direct teaching by others such as teachers, accepted

authority figures, or accepted experts.

- Direct experiences, especially negative ones like past failures, embarrassments, or traumatic experiences.
- Socialization, including the acceptance or rejection from others (perceived or actual).
- Media- tv/movies, social media, content streaming platforms, the internet.
- The "dust bunny effect" of like attracts like. Once your mind-brain has established a negative thought program, it tends to draw in other thoughts and beliefs that reinforce it. Kind of like an electromagnet- once it is turned on, it will pull into itself all other magnetic things. Or the dust bunny under the couch- it will draw more and more dust toward itself such that it can quickly double in size if you do not maintain the amount of unwanted "dust" in your home. In this extended metaphor, the home represents your mind, the dust represents random negative thoughts/beliefs, and the dust bunny represents the culmination of this process into something larger than we expected.

We could certainly further subdivide this list and come up with many other specific examples; however, let us focus on the important takeaway, which is that you understand that all or some of these things can and do significantly form and affect our patterns of thinking and the way in which the brain forms its connections.

After reading this list of how negative thought programs can develop, it may seem that nothing can be done. However, this is simply not true! We absolutely have the power to control our own thoughts! We are the "super-users" or administrators of the system. You can write new programming as a super-user using intentional focus and your natural neuroplasticity. Even regarding genetics, fascinating research is emerging that we can upgrade or downgrade certain genes or genetic expressions using intentional thought (Lipton, 2015)! This truly amazing research crushes the common belief that we have no control over our brain or body simply because of the way we were born!

Some sources of negative thought programs create very dominant or hardwired programs that can constantly affect you, making them quite troublesome and controlling (see Week One about neural networks and neuroplasticity if you need a refresher). The most severe culprit is being exposed to intense fear via trauma, especially when the body's survival mode is activated. If this exposure was repetitive, it means that the fear was reinforced, which strengthens the dominance or hardwiring of the negative thought program.

The brain is really efficient at keeping us alive. Consider for a moment someone in a dangerous or even life-threatening situation. Whether real or anticipated, these situations tell the brain to activate survival mode- fight or flight. In this mode, hardwiring tends to occur quickly. If a person did not learn patterns of thinking and reacting in life-threatening situations very quickly, then they could die. So, the brain is efficient in this respect- looking out for and protecting us. The trouble is when these programs are no longer necessary- when the threat is no longer there, but the programming stays put because fear and survival mode are really effective and efficient ways of producing hardwired networks.

Important Point: Fear

All negative thought programs have some degree of fear in common. Of course, there are countless other negative emotions, like anger, sadness, or jealousy, just to name a few, but many experts believe those are all products or subtypes of one big culprit: fear.

Consider for a moment whether we would likely experience anything else negative in the absence of fear. No. Not likely. The absence of fear allows for positive experiences like peace, happiness, and harmony, not other negative emotions. Thus, we really want to hone in on fear because it is either the root cause of everything else negative or something that, when gone, also cancels the opportunity for other sources of negativity.

Whether you believe negative thoughts and emotions are separate or just different versions or manifestations of fear, being in a constant state of fear or other negativity, such as anxiety, stress, anger, sadness, etc., is very unhealthy! Living in a negative state constantly activates the body's sympathetic nervous system (survival mode or "fight or flight"), which is similar to what happens with trauma. Even though the intensity level might not be as great, the result is still bad. Unfortunately, many people live day to day in this mode. It takes a huge toll on the body and causes us to feel awful a lot of the time. Feeling good, happy, or positive is impossible when our brain and body are locked in survival mode.

Ok- so we learned some examples of sources of negative thought programs; now let me give you some examples of types of negative thought programs. They often tell us:

- We are no good at anything.
- Things never go our way.

- Other people do not like us, so we should be more like someone else.

- To seek approval and validation from others.

- If people disagree with us, they are wrong, bad, or trying to harm us.

- Things will never get better.

- We need certain things or to do certain things for everything to be alright or better.

- To believe bad things about others.

- Not to trust anyone.

There are countless others. I once began a list of all the different negative thought programs people experience, but it was very long and not fun to focus my attention on. While we often share types of negative thought programs with others, our minds individualize them to fit into the circumstances of our own lives. They have specific wording for each person.

Most negative thought programs are irrational, meaning there is not much truth to them, or they are a distorted version of the truth. But that is not always the case. I get this question a lot: "But what about the negative thought programs that are true?" For example, what if something bad did happen once? Maybe even more than once? And the person became fearful of this real thing that actually happened? Is that not a logical reason to be anxious? The answer is yes- when something bad happens, especially if it happened more than once, it is likely a rational or logical reason to be fearful. However, does that mean you continually want that experience? Of course not. We do not want to be stuck with any negative programming, whether it is the result of something that really happened or not.

Important Point: Counterintuitive Logic

It might sound counterintuitive or contrary to logical sense, but it is often irrelevant where your negative thought programs came from or why. People can get fixated or stuck on this topic, inadvertently seeking out and reinforcing negative things that should not have their attention! The exception is when there are genuine problems that need resolution. In this case, working with a therapist is necessary to ensure you are not getting "stuck."

Which types of negative thoughts do you tend to experience? Do you notice certain ones seem to be stronger or more dominant than others?

Now that you have identified some of your negative thought programs, it is useful to be an excellent detective and root out the layers. Doing so will give you greater insight and command over the contents of the negative mind!

In Week One, I mentioned how negative thought programs actually influence the development of neural networks in the physical brain. These neural networks do not exist in isolation. They form complex networks that connect all over the brain. At the beginning of this chapter, I also explained the dust bunny/electromagnet effect, which means that negative thought programs will attract other similar content for reinforcement. This is analogous to the layers of an onion, programming with subprogramming, or a branching tree limb.

Technique: Running a Mind Diagnostic

I would like you to consider a technique that I call "Running a Mind Diagnostic." It is a structured journaling exercise that involves only observing and reporting your thought contents. It is a bit higher level than what you have done so far, but reveals a lot of information! When I work with adults, I insist they thought journal.

It requires you to devote about a week to keeping your journal or journaling device nearby. This is because you will pick it up and write intermittently, not all day. You are to pay attention to when a negative thought program becomes active (usually when you are triggered, but we know from earlier it can also occur during downtimes), identify the program's wording, and then write down everything else that follows. And believe me, there is plenty that follows!

You are not to interact with, judge, or censor the thoughts. Just observe and report because you are only looking for information, mind-data if you will. Avoid adding details like how you feel about situations or stories about your day. Follow the branching effect of the thoughts from one to the next until they seem to stop or enter a repeating loop.

After you have decided to be done with this exercise, reread your journal. If you devoted sufficient time to this, your journal should be pretty full. Notice common themes or repetitive content, including specific wording such as "I can't, I never, I hate", etc. Make a note of these at the end of your journal. These are the negative programs residing in your mind-brain, dictating how you feel, behave, and experience your world. You might be surprised at the content of these negative thought programs. They can be ridiculous but also ruthless! But once you expose them, they begin to lose power over you.

Important Point: Defensive Firewalls

The negative programming of the mind-brain can be defensive. It can have what I call "firewalls" or defensive reactions to keep us from discovering and bringing it into the light. If you are doing your detective work and then suddenly experience anger or irritability at the process, self-judgment over the thoughts you are uncovering, physical symptoms like a headache or stomach ache, or a sudden blanking of the mind (I call this the "blank slate"), then you have likely just come across a defense system trying to thwart you, distract you, and make you go away. This is like in the movie The Wizard of Oz when the wizard is booming at Dorothy and her friends while Toto is off to the side, pulling back the curtain, exposing that the wizard is just a man hiding behind a curtain trying to scare and fool people. If you encounter a firewall or defensive reaction- just know that it cannot harm you and that it is actually a sign you are onto something important! All you have to do is pull back the curtain to see how powerless the negative becomes once you expose it.

Technique: Interview with the Negative

Another useful technique I recommend for uncovering negative thought programs is something I call "Interview with the Negative." It is slightly different than the thought journaling exercise in that you will be more interactive with the negative thoughts, although in a neutral way.

The Interview with the Negative exercise is very useful for getting at the root of a program, preventing you from succumbing to the thinking. Here is how you do it: As soon as you become aware of a negative thought program coming online, begin to interrogate it or ask it questions. Just like a detective would to a suspect! The negative thought program is your suspect.

Ask it (out loud or silently), "What is it that you want me to believe?" Then, be still for a moment. You will get a response. The response usually comes in the form of an impression, a feeling, or a thought popping into your head. You may suddenly feel like you "know" the answer. This part takes a little practice and the response is a bit different for everybody. But do not worry; there is always a response!

Now, for demonstration purposes, let us play out a pretty typical interview with the negative:

Negative: "You should be nervous about going to school today."

You: "Hmmm, that's interesting. Why should I be nervous?"

Negative: "Well, yesterday, that kid was mean to your friend about her clothes."

You: "So what?"

Negative: "You are wearing your new shirt today."

You: "And?"

Negative: "He will probably make fun of you, too."

You: "I see."

Negative: "Best to be worried and either not wear it or do what you can all day to avoid this from happening to you. You should probably not think of anything else and start planning now."

You: "Wow, that's a lot of worry. Anything else?"

Negative: "Yeah, if you get made fun of, you will never recover. It will follow you for the rest of your life. You can't handle these sorts of things."

You: "Reallllly? Anything else?!"

Negative: "You can't handle a lot of things, and other people know it. You are always at risk of being made fun of. Best to get worrying and planning for the worst-case scenario."

You: "Okay, what else do you think you have over me today?"

Negative: "That should do it for now. But stay tuned; I have plenty of material."

You: "Interesting."

Notice how ridiculous this negative program sounds when approached in this manner! However, when it plays out silently in the back of our minds, we tend to become engaged and go along with it.

Notice also in the above dialogue that you stay disengaged. Never buy what the negative is selling! Only prompt the negative with simple, neutral-type questions, known as open-ended questions.

Open-ended questions allow the other party (the negative) to freely provide details without you inadvertently leading it in one direction or another. You are simply looking for information while getting the negative to spill its guts under the spotlight of your interrogation! Sometimes, this can be a long interview because the negative likes to take you all over the place! But that is okay! Just stay with it and follow along as a curious observer, quietly making note of everything it has to say ("Ahaaa, Hmmmm, Interesting, What else?, Then what?, So what?").

This technique is very helpful for avoiding the "mind trap" of aligning with the negative. A mind trap is when the negative bests you with its tactics, getting you to go along with its train of thought so that you essentially turn on yourself without realizing it.

The open-ended style of interrogating the negative shifts you into a different relationship position with the negative, allowing you to see it from a more detached perspective where you have the authority. It helps prevent you from immediately agreeing with it and, therefore, knee-jerk reacting to it. It changes the balance of power, known as a "paradigm shift," which I will discuss in greater detail in Week Four.

Keep track of your interview results, preferably by writing them down, but you can also voice record yourself. Later, when you get really good at this technique, you can do it in your head but journaling is always recommended, especially if you have the time and something to write with when it happens. I use this technique myself when I experience a trigger and am having difficulty identifying its source!

Try out the "Interview with the Negative" and write your responses below:

WEEK THREE

Focus of the Week:

Our third week focused on identifying the specific negative thought programs running in your mind! I explained the various sources of these programs, from genetics and upbringing to social media and what I call the "dust bunny effect," where negative thoughts attract more negative thoughts. While these sources may seem daunting, remember that you are the superuser of your mind-brain and can absolutely use your skills to wield control!

I emphasized an important point: **all negative thought programs share fear as their common denominator.** When we live in constant fear or negativity, our brain stays locked in survival mode, making it impossible to feel good or positive.

To help you detect and understand your negative thought programs, I introduced two powerful techniques: "Running a Mind Diagnostic" and "Interview with the Negative." These structured approaches help you observe, document, and interrogate your negative thoughts, ultimately exposing them and reducing their power over you. Try them for the week. They are tools to help you gain deeper insight into your mind and take control of your thinking patterns.

Week Four

Rejection and Separation

Now that you have expanded your awareness, rooted out, and identified the negative thought programs impacting you, it is time to do something with this information!

Rejection

You must reject the identified negative thought programs in an intentional manner. You cannot shift into a position of greater control without being deliberate about your actions.

Technique: Rejection

Declare (silently or out loud- but out loud has more oomph): "I reject this thinking/these thoughts because I understand how the mind works! I understand that whatever my mind is focused on, or wherever my attention is placed, is what I will inevitably experience. I know that my mind-brain will activate neural networks that will cause me to experience these negative thoughts. And I know that I do not want to experience these negative thoughts. Therefore, I declare that I reject them!"

Declaring that you reject the thoughts is the first step in taking control of your mind-brain and, therefore, your experiences (emotions and behaviors). It seems like such a small thing, but it is not! It is the beginning stages of the paradigm shift between you and your mind-brain.

A paradigm shift is when something previously considered the truth of the way things are is no longer the case, a major change in previously established ways of understanding. This paradigm shift essentially takes the power away from the negative thoughts (that you believed up to this point you could not control), and places the power in your hands. Empowering!

Separation

Next, you must separate yourself and create distance from negative thinking.

Most people believe that they are the same thing as their negative thoughts/thinking! People have told me countless times, "It's just me, it's just the way I think." or "It's just the way my brain works, I can't do anything about it," or various other versions of these types of statements.

Additionally, people identify, relate to, or align with these thoughts. They agree with them! They go along with the thinking! This is especially true when the negative mind brings up actual events. For example, "I failed the last couple of times, so why try anymore? I am no good at anything; things just don't work out for me."

WEEK FOUR

Here, the person agrees with this thinking and even views it as rational or logical simply because it is true that something did not work out before- as if that is the only outcome possible! I mentioned earlier how the negative mind loves to use evidence against us to reinforce itself. It loves to find real-life reasons to prove to you that the way it is thinking is the correct way. Falling for this so-called evidence is a mind trap.

Here is another mind trap: Sometimes, people not only align with negative thoughts but also own them, wearing them like a badge of honor. Owning negative thinking is dangerous because it prompts defensiveness at the idea of getting rid of it. The negative mind will always attempt to defend itself against a perceived threat (recall my earlier explanation about it having a defense system?) I know it sounds crazy, but it happens!

For example, sometimes people believe that living through bad things is necessary for "earning" something, like achieving credibility through suffering. Another belief is that suffering is necessary for learning, self-advancement, or even that God will look favorably upon you for it! You must trust me on this one- God does not want you to suffer or be in pain! That is the opposite of anything positive, especially love. The only outcome of falling for this mind trap is to block yourself from realizing happiness.

At any rate, owning negative thinking is dangerous because it involves melding your identity, or who you believe you are, with the negative thing. People stuck in this trap typically talk openly about their pain or negative experiences, and quite often, when you encounter someone like this, it will not be long before they tell you of their suffering. Sometimes, it can even seem like they are boasting or competing with you for who has it worse!

When I meet people like this, they often become quite defensive at the suggestion that they can be rid of their suffering if they choose to learn about how the mind-brain works. I have been told things such as, "Oh, noooo! But I have depression (or insert any type of diagnosis)! I have had it for many years. It's how my brain works. My doctor told me I have a chemical imbalance and that I have to take medication for it. I just want to learn how to cope with it better."

Essentially, what this person's negative mind is shouting at me is, "Back off! How dare you suggest taking away "my" depression (pain/suffering). It's mine! I earned it! I need it to know who I am. I won't let you "change" me! I just need to cope better." I am certain you can see how bad this mind trap is. Beware because it is nasty!

A Note About Coping

I need to digress for a moment and give my opinion about coping. With respect to achieving a growth mindset and having control over your mind-brain, "cope" is a four-letter word to me! Here is why: Coping means learning ways to deal with what you do not like by accepting that you have no power to change anything other than how you react to what troubles you.

Allow me to illustrate: Imagine living in a house that you do not like. It may not be that nice, it may need a lot of repairs, or

WEEK FOUR

there may even be big holes in the roof. And then- it starts to rain! "Coping" is learning how to get some buckets, put a tarp on the roof, and repeat to yourself, over and over, that it is not that bad until you convince yourself to live in a house you cannot stand being in.

I disagree with this. You do not have to live in a house that you do not like. You can live in whatever house you want to. But you have to build it. No one can do that for you. You actually have to get up off that yucky sofa in the leaky house and walk out of it. Then, you must use the resources you have to create what you want. You cannot "cope" your way out of it. And you certainly cannot expect to "earn" your way out by attaching your identity to negative thinking and experiences like pain and suffering. The house is a metaphor for your mind and you do not need to settle for one that works against you. I will teach you the skills, but you have to do the building... and you are totally capable of doing so!

You do not need to settle for coping

Technique: Separation

Once you have become aware of, identified, and actively rejected a negative thought program, it is time to separate yourself from it!

Declare (silently or out loud- but out loud has more oomph): "I am not these thoughts! Just because I hear or am aware of them does not mean I am them! It does not mean I have to do them, agree with them, be them, or anything else. They have no power to make me do or believe anything. In fact, I am my own person! I get to decide what I go along with. I get to choose what I agree with, what I believe, and what I want to experience!"

How about that for logic and turning the tables on what controls you? It is mission-critical that we distance ourselves from the negative. When we realize that we can view negative thoughts as just unwanted noise that has no authority over us whatsoever, the dynamics of power start to shift back to you—the super-user.

Once you have declared that you and the negative thought programs are not one and the same, there are several more useful techniques from which to choose that will assist you in gaining even more ground.

Technique: Visualize The Negative

Imagine that you could visualize the negative. If these negative thoughts had a shape, a form, a color, or an appearance, what would you see?

For example, some people have described envisioning a black cloud following them around and raining or storming over them. Some people describe a blobby-looking thing that lurks around and jumps out at them when they least expect it. Another example was someone who described a black gooey thing like bubble gum stuck to her that was hard to pick off because of how sticky it was. Whatever you envision your negative thinking to appear as– use your new-found personal power to confront and neutralize it!

In the above-listed examples, the person with the storm cloud envisioned the sun dissolving the storm, the person with the lurking blobby thing envisioned laughing at it for being so silly and childish as to hide around corners, and the person with the gooey-gummy thing envisioned simply washing it off with a powerful anti-sticky cleaner! Whatever you envision as the negative, I can guarantee that your positive mind is waiting in the wings with the neutralizing antidote! Use it! Later- I will tell you more about visualization, but for now, just know that visualization is an extremely powerful tool you should always use.

What would you visualize your negative to appear like, and how would you neutralize it? Feel free to draw!

Technique: Dealing with Trauma-Based Reactions

As stated earlier, traumatic experiences can, unfortunately, create quite a bit of hardwiring that triggers strong physical responses like a pounding heart, difficulty breathing, uncontrollable crying, or shaking. Some people even feel fuzzy, distant, or detached from their bodies. That is the mind-brain's way of protecting you from perceived danger. It is an awful experience. If it ever happens to you, just realize that these physical reactions are the result of stress hormones being released into the body so you can defend yourself or get away from a threat. But when a real threat is no longer present, this reaction is not helpful and commonly becomes what is known an anxiety or panic attack.

After becoming aware of, identifying, rejecting, and separating from the negative thought program, declare (out loud or to self): "You are not from here! You are from another place and another time. You are no longer happening or relevant to me. You are to return immediately to where you came from because you do not belong in the present. You have no power or business here. I reject you!"

Next, use your five senses to pull your attention away from your thoughts. Focus! What is in front of you? What is happening right now? Where are you? What do your surroundings look like? What can you smell? What do some of the things around you feel like? Pick something up and describe it with as many senses as you can. Be as detailed as possible.

Engaging your five senses anchors you to the here and now (the present), which helps slam the door on negative thoughts invading from the past. There are other helpful techniques to keep you present, such as performing mental activities like counting, naming, reciting, or singing. The key is to make the mental activity challenging but not difficult. For example, count backward, skip odd numbers, or make up a song that rhymes. Practicing slow, controlled breathing while counting is also very helpful and benefits the mind and body simultaneously. Counting seconds or breaths helps focus your mind on the present, while slow, rhythmic breathing calms the body. Disciplined breathing, or "breathwork," is a category all on its own, which I will describe in more detail in Week Eight.

If you have symptoms akin to trauma-based reactions, it does not mean you cannot manage them, but you should have additional support. I encourage you to seek assistance from a trusted adult or therapist if you think you might be experiencing trauma-based reactions.

Cognitive Behavior Therapy (CBT)

Cognitive Behavior Therapy (CBT) is an evidence-based treatment focusing on the relationships and patterns of thoughts, emotions, and behavior. Therefore, it is an integral component of the mind-brain approach. Employing CBT techniques is an effective way to reject and separate from the negative. In fact, CBT has been proven to assist with positive changes in neuroplasticity (Appelbaum et al., 2022). Here are a couple that you may have heard of before. There are different types, but I like these the best:

Technique: Thought Challenging

This is when you identify and call out the negative thinking and then challenge and/or dismiss it.

For example, "I am afraid bad things will happen! Bad things always happen to me, so I expect more to happen. I am afraid!" Call out this negative thought and challenge it like you are the best debunker ever! You might respond with something like, "Wow! These thoughts are very loud and negative! It is not even true that bad things always happen to me! I find this thinking ridiculous because I realize that it prevents me from enjoying things I like. It does not help me at all. It just makes me scared. Just because something bad happened before does not mean it will always happen! That does not make sense, and I won't go along with nonsense!"

Technique: Thought Reframing/Neutralizing

This is when you identify the negative thinking and then change it or neutralize it so that it does not have as much negative force behind it. For the above example, one could respond with, "Just because something bad happened before or could happen again does not mean I should be afraid all the time. In fact, even if something bad happens, I know what to do. I am competent. I know where to go and who to talk to. So why should I agree with these thoughts and prevent myself from going somewhere or doing something fun? I am strong, I am learning all about the mind-brain, and I know how to handle myself if something negative happens. Because of this, I refuse to waste another moment on this fearful thinking- it will only limit me."

Important Point: Disengage From the Negative

We generally want to disengage from negative thinking as much as possible. Interacting with it only keeps it active and online, regardless of whether you are refuting or challenging it. Think of arguing with someone. You might be disagreeing with them, but at the same time, you are also actively interacting with them. Ever heard anyone say, "Just walk away?" That is because you cannot stop a conflict by continuing to engage in one.

The same is true for our own negative thinking. We only interact with negative thoughts long enough to identify the content and understand what is happening. The journaling and interview techniques are useful for this purpose because they build insight and awareness through identification. We can then use the basic CBT thought challenging and reframing techniques to help us get our bearings and assist with the paradigm shift. However, we do not want to stall out at this phase of the process and risk getting stuck in an endless cycle of engaging with the negative! We do not want it active!

Over my career, I have worked with many people who have done formal cognitive behavior therapy. They learned how to challenge and neutralize their irrational, negative thinking but later found it exhausting and only helpful in the short term. Why? Unfortunately, for whatever reason, they got stuck in the engagement phase with their negative minds. (Disclaimer- CBT is not just about engaging the negative, although many people overly focus on it). Imagine being constantly embattled with someone with no end in sight! After encouraging them to fight with you by actively engaging them, you would eventually run out of steam- and probably get sucker punched, too! To avoid this, we must pivot away as soon as possible to maintain our position on the high ground.

Think of a time when you experienced some really controlling negative thoughts. How would you reject and separate yourself from these? Which techniques from above would you prefer to use?

Focus of the Week:

Week Four focused on what to do with the negative thought programs you identified! I introduced two critical concepts: rejection and separation. Rejection means intentionally declaring that you refuse to align with negative thoughts, while separation involves creating distance by understanding that you are much more than your negative thoughts. In fact, you are far greater, which is why we never settle for just coping with them!

I explained several mission-critical techniques to help you accomplish this: the basic "Rejection" and "Separation" declarations, "Visualizing the Negative," handling trauma-based reactions through grounding techniques, and using Cognitive Behavioral Therapy (CBT) approaches like thought challenging and reframing. However, I emphasized an important point: While these techniques are valuable, we do not want to constantly engage with negative thoughts. Our goal is to identify them and then pivot away as quickly as possible.

I provided exercises to practice these techniques. Remember, they are not assignments - they are tools to help you gain control over your mind-brain system and shift the balance of power back to you, the superuser!

Week Five

Focal Points

Now that we have applied our new-found skills of rejecting and separating from the negative mind, we must have a different destination for our mind-brain. We need a focal point, a different place for our attention, in order to experience something other than repetitive, negative thoughts. We must now create new, positive thought programs for ourselves so that these become the dominant sources of our experiences!

Imagine driving your car around with the GPS on, trying to get somewhere fun and exciting but without inputting a destination. You would have a haphazard, random experience. You would observe yourself driving and eventually get somewhere, although it may not be the kind of place where you really want to be. This clearly does not make any sense, yet we tend to do it with respect to our thinking. So, let us hone in on a destination of the mind!

Technique: Mantras and Affirmations

Choose three positive describing terms or words that you want to be able to experience every day as a normal part of your life. These are your focal points. You are not limited to three, but I recommend starting here so it is manageable while you are in the initial learning phase.

You can and should change or adjust these as often as you see fit, but do not jump around! Doing so causes you to be inconsistent and lack focus on a destination, resulting in a poorly constructed foundation for your new thought programs. Choose a few, develop them, and then, as you progress, you can and should build other ones.

Your chosen focal point can be emotions or things. For example, many people commonly pick happiness or peacefulness, which are great. But you could also choose things like love, health, wealth, knowledge, strength, self-competence, being a magnet for all good things, or anything else you want to experience every day as a "new normal." The sky is the limit, and it is totally up to you! Remember- this is the foundation for building new, positive mind-brain networks to provide you with more positive life experiences. You are an individual with your own unique life circumstances, so be specific!

First, you will begin using these focal points as mantras and affirmations. Mantras are short phrases you say to yourself, over and over, kind of like a self-command. An affirmation is using the same words but in a longer statement that is also positive, in the present, and something you possess. For extra power, add the words "I know." Think of this like a coding exercise to program a computer by entering the data into the prompt, except the computer is actually your mind-brain.

Here is an example of how to use the emotion of happiness in mantra form: "Happiness. I am happy. I feel happy." In affirmation form, it could be: "I experience happiness all the time. Happiness is in my life now. I am so relieved to know I can be happy, have happiness, and experience happiness." You must declare that you are happy, have happiness, and that it is happening to you now. Add that you "know" it for extra oomph.

We use mantras and affirmations because this is how the negative programs work. We are not reinventing the wheel! We will be using the same processes only to our benefit. For example, when we experience angry feelings or demonstrate angry behaviors, it is because a negative mind-brain program has been activated, telling us to feel angry, even if we do not realize it right away: "I am so angry. He makes me so mad. I know that I have a right to be angry! I feel like exploding!" I am sure you have already uncovered similarly phrased content during Week Three's identification exercises. Now, remember that whatever the mind-brain is focused on and "streaming" to you over and over is eventually what you will experience.

Write down three positive describing terms/ phrases that you will use in mantra and affirmation format. How will you word these?

Important Point: External vs Internal

The mind-brain does not differentiate between something actually happening in our external world or something happening only in our internal world to deliver us the coinciding experience. This is exactly what anxiety is about. An event triggers the anxiety or fear program. Then it begins repeating something to the effect of, "You are anxious, you have anxiety, you are afraid right now!" What happens after that negative mantra and affirmation have been on a loop? That is right- you become anxious and fearful because your physical brain starts complying with these commands, providing you with the matching experience regardless of whether anything fearful or anxiety-producing is actually going on around you.

Technique: Narrative and Visualization

Next, you will build a narrative or a storyline about your focal points to repeat to yourself. You will also need to visualize it! You must be able to "see" it in a way that you can connect to. You are visualizing the feelings and experiences that you want to have. You should choose a real-life event representing one of your positive focal points.

Important Point: Large vs Small Events

The mind-brain does not differentiate or assign more

importance to large, monumental events over small, personal situations. Often, people tell me, "But I am not happy. I want to be, but that's the problem. I don't experience happiness, so I can't come up with anything." You do not need to come up with a major life-changing event. It can be a smaller personal circumstance as long as you can connect to the real-life experience by recalling the feeling and seeing yourself having the experience of your focal point.

For example, perhaps when you go for a walk in the park or down a nature trail, you pass by some beautiful trees or flowers, and you realize that just by seeing those things, you feel happy, even for a moment. Or perhaps you really like ice cream, and you know that after dinner, you are going to get to have your favorite kind. And the thought of that makes you happy. The point is that you are connecting yourself to the actual experience you want, knowing that your thoughts, feelings, and behaviors will eventually match whatever you have set as the primary focal point for your mind-brain.

The narrative might go something like this: "I have happiness in my life. I know that I am capable of happiness. In fact, I choose to walk down that nature trail several times a week because I love being in that section of the park! The nature is so beautiful, and I feel so happy just being there!" This narrative supports and reinforces your mantras/affirmations and provides a real-life experience to connect to and visualize.

GROWTH MINDSET

If you absolutely cannot come up with any real-life experiences of your positive describing term, then you can create something you really connect with. Make sure you can visualize it just as well as a memory of a real-life event because it needs to be as if you are experiencing it.

Write your narrative. Include enough detail so it is rich with imagery but not so complicated that you cannot recall what you came up with!

Important Point: The Power of Visualization

Visualization is a powerful tool for programming the mind-brain. It activates the same neural networks and processes of the brain as if we were having the actual experience! This allows our powers of neuroplasticity to kick in, making changes to our neural patterns and, thus, our overall experiences without actually having to do anything physical.

Studies have shown that visualization is particularly effective when practiced from the first-person perspective as if you were actually there experiencing your visualization. If you adopt an outside observer perspective as if you were watching a movie, it still works, but not to the same degree. Additionally, it has been concluded that there is a causal relationship between visualization and emotions- it is not just a correlation (Burnett Heyes, Pictet, Mitchell, Raeder, Lau, Holmes, ... Blackwell, 2017). This is why we must intentionally immerse ourselves in and "feel" our visualizations. It means a more efficient and effective process of self-programming.

Research conducted by Velikova, Sjaaheim, and Nordtug (2017) determined that when a person uses visual imagery in a self-guided manner with specific intention based on an identified need, they can achieve positive emotional changes.

Heyes, Lau, and Holmes (2013) found that visualization exercises should always be purposeful and relevant to the skills sought after, especially during childhood development.

Speaking to the power of vivid mental imagery, Dijkstra and Fleming (2021) conducted a study to determine if the brain can differentiate between mental imagery and real images. Their results revealed that the more vivid a person's mental imagery is, the more the brain perceives it as real. They stated (para. 336), "...these results also suggest that if imagery does become vivid or strong enough, it will be indistinguishable from perception."

Now, you can see why paying attention to strong, repetitive, negative thinking is not good. As its storyline plays out, your focus and attention become hijacked with its strong mental imagery, entrapping you in a negative experience!

Draw what you imagine for your positive visualization in any way you want! You do not have to be an artist!

Technique: Sleep-Wake Routine

Waking up and going to sleep are times of the day when we have the most natural access to and influence over the subconscious mind. Recall that the subconscious mind contains volumes of content we are trying to become more aware of. These are the times of day when our mind-brain transitions between the awake (conscious) state and the sleep (subconscious) state. The subconscious mind is accessible during these times. We always want to take advantage of what is naturally available to us!

In the morning, as soon as you are aware you are waking up, do not open your eyes. Just lay there and begin your chosen positive mantras/affirmations, narrative, and visualizations. Slowly open your eyes and repeat again while becoming fully awake. Set an intention to expect a day full of positive experiences. Acknowledge that you are entering new programming directly into your subconscious mind and pressing the "play" button to have positive programming running in the background all day.

Important Point: Expect Positive Experiences

Expecting positive experiences keeps you optimistic and opens you to opportunities. Most people believe that focusing on worst-case scenarios will prepare them for let-downs or disappointments when, in reality, it only programs an intention to expect disaster. These types of thought programs provoke fear-based networks in the brain, causing a cascade of negative experiences like pessimism, apprehension, hypervigilance, exhaustion, irritability, and stress.

When it is bedtime, get excited! Tell yourself that you cannot wait to get in bed because you get to imagine everything positive that you want for yourself. Connect to and feel it! You are providing the material for your subconscious to integrate with your mind-brain while you sleep. Go to sleep repeating and imagining your mantras/affirmations, narratives, and visualizations.

Never go to bed in a negative state, watching TV, scrolling the internet, or playing video games! You will inadvertently program your subconscious mind with the contents of your attention. This does not bode well for a peaceful night's sleep. Going to bed or waking up with negativity undermines your progress and is actually a form of self-sabotage!

In sum, develop your positive describing words into mantras and affirmations, then add narratives with visualizations you can feel! Press play as often as possible, but definitely upon waking up or going to sleep. Consistency is mission-critical! You have just begun the foundational aspects of creating new, positive, hardwired programming for yourself.

Focus of the Week:

Week Five focused on creating new, positive thought programs to replace the negative ones. Just like the GPS in your car needs a destination to direct you where you want to go, your mind also needs a clear direction. I introduced several techniques to help you program positive experiences into your mind-brain.

I showed you how to develop mantras and affirmations using three positive describing terms, create rich narratives and visualizations, and establish a sleep-wake routine that takes advantage of your naturally accessible subconscious mind. An important point I emphasized is that your mind-brain does not differentiate between external and internal experiences - so visualizing positive experiences can be just as powerful as living them!

I provided exercises to help you practice these techniques. Remember, these are tools to help you build new neural networks that will create the positive experiences you want to have. Consistency is mission-critical in this process of creating new, positive, hardwired programming for yourself!

Week Six

Shifting

Shifting is the next phase of our journey toward hardwiring new positive thought programs into our mind-brains. It is the act of intentionally moving your conscious awareness from point A to point B—or from the negative to the positive. We always want to shift away from negative thinking because we know that it will cause us to have experiences that align with it.

Imagine watching your TV or whatever device you are using to stream content. You can watch one channel or show but just as easily switch to watching something else. By changing the channel, you have shifted your attention from one thing to another. The first thing that you were watching did not disappear or cease to exist. You simply shifted off of its frequency or wavelength and onto another channel. Now, your attention and focus exist there. You can change the channel to anything you want, but unless you have a specific channel to watch- a specific focal point- you can end up endlessly surfing around. You will eventually land on something, but it might not be exactly what you wanted to watch, and you may have wasted a lot of time in the process.

When we practice intentional thinking, we are really practicing placing our awareness and attention exactly where we want it to be. Hence, the reason I asked you to create the three focal points in Week Five.

You must have a place to "be." A place for your mind-brain to "be from." Whatever channel you have tuned into literally becomes what you are "attuned" to... and we know that the corresponding experiences will come thereafter.

Technique: Shifting with Memory and Attention

Shifting is very simple and only requires memory and attention. You simply recall what you have already created for yourself with your mantras, affirmations, narrative, and visualizing exercises. Recalling these focal points becomes like a "mind destination" for your attention.

WEEK SIX

It only takes a few seconds to begin attuning yourself to the new TV channel metaphor I referenced in Week Five. When you first start this process, you will find that you quickly shift back to the "old channel." This is because the old channel is the hardwired default channel. That is okay. Do not be dismayed or let frustration get the better of you. You are in the process of creating new hardwiring to be your default channel. The bouncing back-and-forth ping-pong ball effect is temporary.

Surprisingly, many people give up at this stage, even though they have already done some of the hardest work! Creating new hardwiring takes conscious intention, repetition, and reinforcement over time. Simply recognize when you have shifted away from where you want to be, and then shift back without assigning negativity or judgment. Just keep shifting! You can maintain your presence where you want it to be with a little practice. Do not give up!

After you get good at shifting, you will only need to self-monitor and self-correct from there on out. The corrections will come much easier because you have a new destination with new programming to "be from." It is just like a computer network. When there is only one network, that is the only one you can use. Nothing else is available- it does not matter if you are unhappy with the current network. But when there is more than one, you can just "throw the switch" and shift onto the network you want to be on. You just have to create it first.

Time Frames

By now, you are probably wondering, "How long does this "hardwiring" process actually take?" Well– the scientific jury is still out, but the general consensus seems to be that the period of time varies from person to person due to all kinds of individual and situational factors. In my experience, I have discovered that about 60 days, eight weeks, or two months is sufficient for just about everyone. Even if it takes a bit longer for you, that is okay!

In 2015, an engineer named Destin Sandlin conducted a really cool experiment. His results were shocking! He found that it took adults about 8 to 12 months to change hardwired neural pathways for riding a bike the normal way so that it could be ridden backward with a set of reverse-engineered handlebars (Arnott, 2024).

The extreme difficulty it posed for people was baffling! An equally baffling discovery was that it was significantly easier for his six-year-old son to do- accomplishing the task in only about two weeks! That is about seven months less time, on the low end of the range! If that is not a testament to the degree of neuroplasticity possessed by young people, I am not sure what is!

In 2019, another researcher named Corbus Oosthuizen tried to accomplish this task by focusing on creating new neural networks instead of wrestling with the established hardwiring. When he used this approach, it only took him 23 minutes and 33 seconds! His method relied on intention, visualization, and mental repetition! Whoa!! (LifeXchange Solutions, 2019).

The takeaway here is clear: Younger people have the advantage over adults regarding natural neuroplasticity, and focusing on generating new neural networks instead of grappling with well-established systems leads to even better results.

Let us translate this information to serve our purposes of shaping the mind-brain to provide the positive experiences we want! If we reflect on the ideal conditions for creating new neural pathways, you already meet those criteria right now! You are both young and have already done the hard work of laying the foundation to create new neural networks. You know not to engage with old, negative, hardwiring. Therefore, you are perfectly poised to succeed!

In sum, you should expect to commit to practicing your skills of intentional focus and repetition for about 60 days. You will need to be as consistent as possible, refocusing yourself without judgment each time you notice the negative becoming an active influence over your thoughts, emotions, or behaviors. You will reinforce your efforts by seeking support from trusted sources and rewarding yourself with praise and admiration for having the GUTS to do this!

As the days progress, by remaining intentionally focused on your positive mind destinations, you will wake up noticing less and less resistance from the negative mind-brain until one day, things just seem to flow.

Important Point: Neutrality

When practicing shifting, we must watch out for a common mind trap of polarized or "only this or only that" thinking. This occurs when the negative mind tells us that if we have not achieved a highly positive state, then we have failed—as if there is nothing in between the absolute negative and the absolute positive!

What about times when something stressful might be happening around you? It might seem a bit inappropriate for the situation to be in an overly positive state. What about times when you have difficulty due to the pong-pong ball effect? This is something that everyone experiences, and it does not indicate failure!

In reality, there is a range of places to "be from." Neutrality is a mind-brain destination where you can manage the negative without being overwhelmed by it.

In a neutral state, you have self-competence and distance from the negative. You have rejected and separated from it. Therefore, you can handle what is happening without succumbing to it. For example, you could shift to a neutral mind-brain destination using a mantra/affirmation such as, "I am competent, I have self-competence, I know how competent I am." Or a narrative such as, "I know this stressful situation is happening, but I also know how to handle myself. I can manage because I have done it before and can connect to that experience. I refuse to fall into a negative mindset. I am able to be in control, just like I have done before. I can shift to a more positive place later, but for now, I am comfortable knowing I am managing."

From a place of neutrality, you can shed off any further influence or effects of the negative and then shift into a more positive state when you are ready. You need not try to "force" yourself into a highly positive state to avoid a negative state.

Think of a recent negative experience you have had. It could be something that happened to you, like an unfortunate event, or something that happened within you, like negative thoughts looping over and over. What could you do to shift away from this? Could you shift directly to one of your positive focal points, or would you need to be in a more neutral position first? Visualize and describe.

Emotions and Energy

Now, let us talk about emotions for a moment. Emotions (or feelings, if you prefer) are experienced both in the thinking mind and the body. Like everything else, emotions are energy. Sometimes, strong, negative emotions make it difficult to shift because their energy gets stuck in our physical body or energy field. This can cause what is commonly known as "blocks." If you have chronic, negative emotions that you just cannot seem to shift away from, you might be experiencing blocked-up energy.

To prevent this from interfering with your personal progress, it is a good idea to establish a routine to "process out" or get rid of pent-up negative emotions. When we do this, we can shift more easily, which naturally causes us to feel better.

Let me first state that experiencing emotions, including negative ones, is a normal part of being human. Also, emotions are transient, which means they flow in and are meant to flow out. It is a natural process.

Unfortunately, when we experience strong, negative emotions, we tend to block the path that they are meant to flow because the feeling is uncomfortable—sometimes even painful. We no longer want to have that experience, so we try to prevent the emotional energy from flowing through us.

Consider positive emotions for a moment, maybe a very strong one like laughter. When we are happy and find something hilarious, we begin to have a physical experience. As the emotion passes through us, our eyes can water, we can have trouble breathing, and our diaphragm even contracts! Yet, I have never met anyone who told me that laughter is a terrible feeling and that they want to avoid it at all costs! Eventually, it drains off naturally, and we return to our previous state. We never think twice about the process of what actually just happened.

Now, let us consider a strong, negative emotion such as rage. When we get triggered into anger, we also begin having a physical experience, but it is not pleasant. Our face can feel hot, our jaw might get tense, and we can have shallow breathing, clenched fists, and tight stomachs. Sometimes, we react to this by trying to prevent it from continuing due to how terrible it feels. This can cause the "bottling-up" of the negative emotion, ultimately keeping it trapped while it builds in intensity.

Eventually, the bottled-up anger will come out, but in an undesirable way, such as through eruptions of rage, exploding on people, or even smashing things. This behavior will not only cause you to feel awful, but it can damage your relationships with others. Additionally, you would have created a bad habit of accumulating blocked, negative energies.

Anger is not the only emotion that causes problems when bottled up; blocking other negative emotions like sadness can lead to depression, blocking guilt can lead to shame, and blocking fear can lead to anxiety or even panic. Bottling up emotions always causes some kind of collateral damage. We also run the risk of anchoring ourselves into negative states for the longer term, which I will describe in greater detail in Week Seven.

Technique: Deal with Negative Emotions

When you start to have an undesirable physical experience of a negative emotion, imagine that you are an open conduit or an open pathway for an energetic charge to pass through. Sometimes, people even prefer to think of a free-flowing river. Tell yourself that all emotions are transient, meant to simply pass through, and as such, this feeling will also pass through. It is only temporary and nothing compared to the experience or consequences of bottling it up.

Concentrate on being "open" and assisting the emotion on its path. There are no kinks or blocks in your conduit, and your river does not have debris or dams. Focus on this visual! Focus on knowing what is actually going on. Focus on thoughts of self-competence—like, "I've got this!" or "I understand what is happening, and I know how to deal with it." This will help reduce the strength of the negative emotion.

If you can, go outside. Stand or sit directly on the ground without shoes. If you have a natural water source nearby, stand or wade in it. The human body has a positive charge, while the earth has a negative one. When we are not connected to the earth, the body can build up a positive charge, which must be discharged to achieve balance. Grounding yourself to the earth will literally assist with draining off of these charged emotions!

This is called "Earthing," and I highly recommend it! Earthing is something that people practice regularly to prevent energy blocks by processing them out of their bodies. Some companies even sell specially designed shoes, clothing, mats, and bedding that assist with keeping you connected to the earth so that you are constantly grounding yourself! Regardless of whether you are a dedicated "Earther," just being outside in nature helps dissipate stuck energies. So- get outside, play, sit on the grass, and maybe even hug a tree!

Imagine a time when you felt a strong, negative emotion. What did your body feel like? Did you try to "bottle up" that energy to prevent yourself from continuing to feel it? How did it affect you?

Focus of the Week:

Our sixth week is complete! Great job staying with it! In this chapter, I introduced shifting - the intentional movement of your conscious awareness from negative to positive thought programs! Using the metaphor of changing TV channels, I explained how you can redirect your attention to your chosen positive focal points, just like switching to a different channel.

I emphasized that it typically takes about 60 days to create new neural pathways but also provided evidence that it can be done much more quickly! Young people have a tremendous advantage because they do not have as much fixed, negative hardwiring as older people. I also introduced the important concept of neutrality—you do not have to jump straight from negative to highly positive states. Sometimes, being in a neutral state is exactly where you need to be.

Finally, I explained how emotions are energy that needs to flow through us. I introduced techniques like visualization and Earthing to help process negative emotions instead of bottling them up. I also provided exercises to practice these concepts, helping you maintain control over where your mind "lives!"

Week Seven

States and Aligned Experiences

What is a State?

A state is an established place of "being from." An established place of thoughts, emotions, and behaviors. If you are in a state of stress, you are being from a home base of stress. It is where you are functioning from.

Refer back to my metaphor in Week Six about the TV channels or even consider radio stations. Imagine you are tuned into just one channel and watch or listen to it constantly. Whatever is on that channel is the frequency or wavelength that you are also on. You will always have the same experiences associated with that channel unless you tune in or attune to a different frequency so you can access a different state. Albert Einstein knew this when he said, "We cannot solve our problems with the same thinking we used when we created them."

I should acknowledge that the exact wording of this statement has been debated, perhaps because it was initially made in his native language of German or because it was not recorded or written when he first said it. However, we understand he spoke about this concept. He was referring to the need to change the channel or get the brain train onto different tracks so as not to perpetuate the same type of problems with the same type of thinking.

This guy might be worth listening to;
he seemed to know a few things!

Important Point: Thoughts vs States

Having negative thoughts or feelings does not necessarily mean you are anchored into a negative state. Experiencing a wide range of thoughts and emotions is a normal part of being human! There is a difference between someone who is feeling down or low for a day and a person who is depressed. The person who is depressed is anchored into an energetic state of depression. They have their tuners locked onto the frequency/channel/station where depression exists.

Here is another example- we all know someone we could describe as a "stressed-out" person. This person thinks, feels, and acts in ways consistent with being attuned to a state of stress. They always seem stressed regardless of whether actual stressful things are going on around them because they are "being from" this state. It becomes the way they view their world. In contrast, stress is a normal human experience. Just because you have a stressful day or feel stressed out does not mean you are anchored into a state of stress.

However, if we allow ourselves to maintain negative thoughts and emotions for long periods of time, we risk inadvertently anchoring ourselves into a negative state. This is why we must always be vigilant. We want to self-monitor and self-correct as soon as possible to avoid getting stuck in a negative state.

States Self-Perpetuate

When we become anchored in a particular mental state, it tends to self-perpetuate through a feedback loop. Our state of mind influences how we perceive and react to experiences, which in turn reinforces that same state of mind.

Consider again the person caught in a state of stress. Their experiences of stress-inducing situations are both real and self-created. Their state causes the mind-brain to overly focus on stress-inducing situations while minimizing or completely ignoring anything that contradicts it! This creates the perception that only bad things are happening. Additionally, another phenomenon occurs- the person actually begins drawing stressful conditions to themselves! If you know anyone like this, you have probably noticed that they, in fact, do have a lot of stress in their lives!

Here is how the cycle works: They begin each day already in a stressed mindset. Throughout the day, they encounter various challenges – perhaps oversleeping because they forgot to set an alarm, arriving late to work, receiving unexpected assignments, or having appointments canceled. While these events are genuine sources of stress, their pre-existing stressed state makes them especially susceptible to and focused on such experiences. Eventually, they become blind to the positive things around them, listening only to the negative programming associated with this state.

Their stressed mindset then uses these events as validation: "This proves everything always goes wrong! Nothing ever works out for me! Why am I constantly faced with problems? No wonder I'm so stressed!" This interpretation strengthens their stress-focused thinking patterns.

Without awareness of this self-reinforcing cycle, they continue believing that external circumstances are the primary source of their stress. In reality, their own thought patterns and emotional responses perpetuate the cycle. They unconsciously create stress through their thoughts, which manifests in their emotions and actions, leading to more stressful experiences.

Imagine driving a car at night. The headlights are shining out in front of you, illuminating the way. You consistently move into what you have illuminated or shined out, and then you have the corresponding experience. You shine out from yourself, then move into that space and have the experience. And so on. This means that our thought programming is causing our experiences. Seeing is not believing- believing is seeing!

Short-Term Effects

Being anchored into a negative state has both short-term and long-term effects. The short-term effects impact things like day-to-day decisions, both small and large, choices, perceptions, and interpretations of events or interactions with others.

Consider a person anchored into an angry state. This person will go through their day "being from" a state of anger. Of course, as we have learned, they will have aligning experiences. They might make rash decisions or choices without careful consideration, leading to undesirable outcomes or completely cancel the chance for positive ones. They might perceive interactions with others or interpret events that happen around them as egregious or against them, which could cause them to spoil relationships or opportunities. It is a snowball effect, and they do not even realize it.

Long-Term Effects

The long-term effects create something known as manifestation. Manifestation occurs when, due to remaining fixed in a particular mental state for an extended period– circumstances, events, people, and situations that match our mental and emotional patterns are drawn to us. We begin to attract what matches our energetic state. People also refer to this as the Law of Attraction.

I have noticed the term manifestation is spoken about quite frequently these days, even in pop culture. Perhaps my experience is due to the state I am anchored into, and I am therefore encountering more things with which I am aligned (see what I did there?). Regardless, this is not a new concept in the least. Many professionals have made careers out of coaching people to think positively and train their mind-brains to attract positive things. Based on what we have covered so far, you know how and why this process works. It is not make-believe.

Manifestation in Professional Practice

In fact, did you know that an entire area of psychology is devoted to manifestation? It is called sports psychology. Sports psychologists are experts at training athletes to control their minds- their awareness and thinking- to draw in success and accomplishments. They rely on the techniques of visualization, positive thinking, acting in alignment, self-monitoring, self-correcting, and extreme focus and attention on the desired outcome to empower elite athletes to achieve their goals. They are essentially practitioners of manifestation techniques- directing athletes to use their mind-brains to achieve great physical feats and accomplishments.

Given that an entire subfield of psychologists does this for a living, and highly accomplished athletes train in this manner, then what I have laid out for you does not seem out of left field, now does it?

Professional business coaches and personal development trainers also rely on these methods to train people to accomplish their or their organization's goals. One of the most famous professionals is a man named Tony Robbins. Over the past several decades, he has trained countless people, including famous people, on how to use their mind-brains to their benefit. He could not possibly have risen to the level that he has if he had only sold lies and duped people.

Important Point: "Dis-ease"

The manifestation of circumstances aligned with the state in which we are anchored does not just apply to external situations. It can also create mental and physical health problems, worsen pre-existing conditions, or make recovery longer than necessary. I call this being caught in a pattern of "dis-ease."

In Week Four, Rejection and Separation, I discussed how people can unwittingly align their sense of self and identity with certain negative thinking and conditions. I used one example of a person with depression becoming defensive at the suggestion of being rid of it. They believed they were the same thing as their thoughts and owned their condition because they had it for so long, and a doctor told them they had a chemical imbalance. Unfortunately, aligning so strongly with this thinking and the corresponding suffering also put this person in a state of depression, which we now know self-perpetuates. Of course, it is possible this person had a predisposition for depression based on genetics or brain chemistry, but their alignment with it canceled opportunities for recovery.

I want to speak for a moment about dis-ease, conditions, or disorders. Simply because you may have been diagnosed or labeled with something does not mean that you must own or identify with it, even if it is due to "brain chemistry" or genetics. In Week Three, I referred to fascinating research by cellular biologist Bruce Lipton, Ph.D. He wrote a book called The Biology of Belief (originally published in 2005, revised 2015) about his findings on cellular genetic expression, among other things. He stated, "The fundamental belief that we are frail, biochemical machines controlled by genes is giving way to an understanding that we are powerful creators of our lives and the world in which we live" (Prologue location 149 of 5786). He further determined that our biology is influenced far more by factors such as environmental conditions and the mind's perceptions than by our genetics. This includes, of course, how we choose to direct our minds to think, feel, and act.

Aligning with disabilities/disorders puts you at risk of anchoring yourself into a state consistent with the negative condition so that your life experiences reflect that condition. Then, you end up going through life, blaming the condition for your experiences. How can you expect to improve or heal from something that you are attuned to and believe you are or possess?

Focus of the Week:

Week Seven explored states - established places of "being from" that determine our thoughts, emotions, and behaviors! Like being tuned to a specific TV channel or frequency, our state determines what experiences we encounter. I explained how states self-perpetuate through feedback loops, creating cycles that can either lift us up or hold us down.

I emphasized that there is a difference between having negative thoughts and being anchored in a negative state. I explained how states can manifest both short-term and long-term effects in our lives. One long-term effect is the concept of manifestation, which involves remaining in a particular state for extended periods and attracting matching circumstances. I also referenced how sports psychologists and other professional coaches and trainers actually teach manifestation principles!

Finally, I explained the concept of "dis-ease" and how aligning too strongly with negative conditions can keep you anchored in unwanted states. Remember - you are not your diagnosis or condition. You are the powerful creator of your experiences through your chosen state of being!

Week Eight

Anchoring

Anchoring is the act of maintaining your presence where you want it to be and, thus, having experiences that are consistent with that state.

There are two types: Internal and External Anchoring.

Internal Anchoring

Internal anchoring is defined as all of the solid, internal work you have done so far—the thinking work, the mindfulness work, the visualization work, the understanding and learning work of how the mind affects the brain, how the brain creates physical structures known as neural networks to provide us with experiences consistent with our repetitive thoughts, and how neuroplasticity enables you to control your own experiences. You have done a lot of internal work!

External Anchoring

External anchoring is the last yet very impactful process required to create new, positive, and lasting experiences for yourself. It involves reducing "exposures" to negative influences and adding actions to support your internal work. Doing so propels your progress forward, causing a catalyst effect with respect to neuroplasticity.

I break this category down further into two subtypes: Exposures and Actions.

Exposures

It is mission-critical that you ensure that whatever you are exposing yourself to or are exposed to daily is as aligned with what you want for yourself as possible. While we cannot always control exposures, we must do our best to minimize any that may be in direct conflict with what we want for ourselves.

Media

Media is one of the biggest examples of exposure problems. It typically only provides negative information that provokes fear, anger, and sadness. Media content almost exclusively focuses on all things bad or wrong in the world. When people say that they want to feel more peaceful or happy but then consume large amounts of news media daily, they are undermining their efforts by exposing themselves to exactly what they do not want to experience. This, of course, only reinforces the negative.

Please read your news if you want to keep abreast of current events! Watching media or TV can have a hypnotic effect on the mind. There is a reason that TV shows/channels used to be called "programming." Make sure that you are the only one in control of that programming! When you read the news, you get

WEEK EIGHT

to scan the information, decide what is important, and choose what to read further about. You have more control, and reading is also good for you! Please avoid subjecting yourself to someone else's "programming" at all costs.

Another good example is a person who wants to work on being more confident or improving their self-esteem but then constantly watches or scrolls through social media. Again, this is a direct contradiction to what one actually wants, and it will only cancel out all of your hard internal work. I have never been a fan of social media, and when I do have to use it, you can guarantee that I am practicing limiting my exposure!

Video gaming or phone games are another example. If someone wants to learn to be more mindful, present, and less reactive but constantly exposes themselves to addictive video games that are designed to entrap the mind-brain, create impulsivity, and generate anger, then, well, you know the outcome.

Important Point: Making Behavioral Changes

It is much easier to make behavioral changes by replacing an unwanted behavior with a more desirable one instead of just trying to quit. For example, if you find yourself watching too much YouTube or spending too much time on social media, replace the negative content with things you are positively aligned with. You do not need to quit YouTube entirely, but be mindful of what you expose yourself to! Replace watching poor content with pursuing content about your hobbies, interests, and the topics of your self-work.

I do not like social media or gaming at all! More data is always coming out about how addictive the algorithms, programs, and visual imagery have been designed to be. Social media is pretty much one big competition for negative attention-seeking and advertising, so try to steer clear entirely. Gaming, especially games with violent content, activates regions in the brain that correspond with violence. It does not matter to your brain whether it is real life or a game, which is a major point I have made throughout this book. The brain responds to what it is programmed with, and the media/gaming people know this!

There are so many other, more positive things that you could be engaging in. I always recommend a social media/gaming fast for two weeks. That means NO social media and NO gaming for two weeks (this includes phone app games). Everyone to whom I recommend this always provides favorable feedback that typically revolves around not being aware of how terrible it made them feel until they stopped using it. I literally have never encountered anyone who told me their life became more negative without social media or gaming!

Other people

Other people are another example of exposure problems. We cannot always control this, but we need to be able to minimize our exposures.

Avoid negative people or people who are in direct conflict with what you want for yourself as much as possible. Sometimes, people tell me that they have a "friend" who drives them crazy or that they do not even like that much, yet they feel obligated to spend time with them. More commonly, people find themselves in friend groups that feel unsupportive, shallow, or even critical - but remain to avoid feeling alone.

Consider the company you keep. Be honest. Are these people authentic? Do these relationships enrich your life and contribute to the positive experiences you want for yourself? Or are they fraught with conflict and pettiness that drains your energy and activates negative thought programs about your self-concept? Remember, the negative mind is always seeking reinforcement, so if you are exposing yourself to low-quality social networks, then you are providing it opportunities to continue controlling you with its destructive narratives.

It is an important, albeit tough, truth in life that we become reflections of the people we choose to spend time with. Every person you welcome into your inner circle either strengthens or weakens your well-being. While it might feel uncomfortable to be selective about friendships, the quality of these connections directly shapes your daily experiences and growth. Yes, finding genuine connections takes time, and you may end up with just a few close friends rather than a large social circle. But one authentic friendship that uplifts and supports your growth is worth far more than a bunch of superficial connections that will only serve to reinforce negative patterns. Even choosing to spend some time alone can be more enriching than engaging in relationships that drain your spirit and feed those harmful thought programs you are working hard to overcome. It is fine to have many acquaintances, but be mindful about who deserves to earn a position in your life.

Aside from peers, other people, such as family members and co-workers, also fall into this category. Sometimes, there is nothing we can do about this. So, always minimize the exposures as much as possible and have an exit strategy. If you must visit that one super-negative relative during the holidays, plan for it! Decide how much time you can realistically manage without being adversely affected, and have a deadline. Stay positive, wish them well, but say that you have another commitment or visit to make and can only stay for a specified period of time.

Do this with negative classmates or co-workers as well. Plan ahead and minimize your exposures as much as possible. Other people's negative energy is very toxic and absolutely has an adverse impact on us.

Identify any exposure problems you may have. Who or what are they? What can you do to reduce or eliminate them? Are there replacements you could make?

Actions

This is a big one! I call it "Doing the Do's." You must DO life in a way that supports and reinforces exactly what it is you have decided you want for yourself. You must pair action-based measures with your intentional thinking skills, essentially solidifying new hardwiring through multiple sources and types of reinforcement.

Your routines, behaviors, decisions, and actions must align with the positive thought programs (and ultimately experiences) that you are in the process of creating. Actions and doing the do's are catalysts for progress. They launch you forward. You can have all the internal work down pat, but if you are taking actions that contradict this, you will be stuck in place, spinning your wheels– ultimately working against yourself.

Adding a ton of new things to your plate is unnecessary. Start by analyzing how you spend your time every day. What are your routines? What kind of schedule do you keep? You can swap out unwanted behaviors or habits with new, more positive, and interesting ones. Starting with a few changes will make it much more manageable and allow you to decide what "Do's" are the most effective for you.

For example, take a person who wants more peace and stability because their life feels hectic, haphazard, or out of control. This person may have done the important internal anchoring work but is not realizing much success. Upon closer inspection, we find that this person maintains routines and behaviors that undermine what they actually want for themselves! They wake up late every morning, rushing from task to task, just trying to get out the door on time. They skip breakfast or a healthy routine of even ten minutes of meditation. They do not exercise. They drive very fast to work, worrying about being on time. They complain or gossip to others. You get the picture. How could this person possibly make any progress when they are essentially canceling or nullifying all of their internal work? This is called self-sabotage.

Write a list below of how you spend your time each day from the moment you wake up until you go to sleep. Do you notice any routines or behaviors that might undermine your progress? If so, what could you do about this?

Important Point: Mind-Brain and Body Harmony

One necessary action that we all must undertake to support our alignment and ensure our success is adopting a regular practice that assists in balancing and harmonizing the relationship between the mind-brain and body. We need to keep the lines of communication and energy open and flowing between them and also ensure that the mind is the one providing the orders to the brain and body, not the other way around. Let us get the direction of our chain of command correct!

Simply practicing positive thinking is not enough to rewire deeply ingrained thought patterns. Our mind and brain work as an interconnected system, with the subconscious mind harboring our most deeply rooted thought patterns below our conscious awareness. These ingrained patterns can trigger physical reactions in our bodies even without obvious external causes.

To create lasting positive change, we must address both the physical responses of our body and the defensive mechanisms of our subconscious mind—what we might think of as its "firewall."

Clearing Persistently Negative Thought Programs

Persistently negative thought programs can create blocks in the subconscious mind and the body's energy field. To clear them, it is important to use mind-body practices that keep our energies and intentions flowing through all aspects of ourselves. Two of my personal favorites are Breathwork and the Emotional Freedom Technique (EFT). Both are evidence-based, with substantial references and resources available on the internet, in books, and in podcasts.

Technique: Breathwork

Breathwork checks all of my boxes! It is a term to describe various types of deliberate breathing patterns and routines. Some techniques are slow and steady, while others involve the practice of very active and sometimes odd-looking ways of inhaling and exhaling. Breathworks is much more than just counting slowly while breathing; it is one of the only practices I insist people try! It is an essential rescue remedy for anxiety or panic attacks because it is highly effective at quieting the negative mind, calming the brain as well as the body, aligning our energies, and bringing immediate relief! It is a must-have for anchoring techniques, and since you are already breathing, why not just try some breathwork? You will not be disappointed!

Technique: The Emotional Freedom Technique (EFT)

EFT is evidence-based, very simple, and involves tapping your fingers on specific points on your hand, head, chest, and ribs in sequence while simultaneously stating affirmations. The points you tap on are meridian or energy points for the body.

When you do this while making positive self-statements, you are clearing those energy points of any blocks, helping to increase your power over the negative contents in your subconscious mind and relax your body simultaneously. Since you are doing mantras/affirmations and positive narratives anyway, why not just tap them in? It does not take any more time, and you are just adding more power to your punch against negative thoughts! Additionally, once you have "tapped in" your new, positive thoughts, you can activate the beneficial effects later by discreetly tapping on the side of your hand. You do not have to go through the entire tapping sequence again!

33 More Anchoring Techniques- Appendix

Low on strategies for anchoring? Do not worry; I have included a list of 33 more in the appendix section! I want you to have a catalog of different techniques to ensure that you engage in productive internal and external anchoring. In this way, you can increase your ability to maintain your presence exactly where you want it by anchoring to the state that you want to be in. Try some from different categories, even if you think you may not like them. You might be surprised how effective going outside of your comfort zone can be!

GROWTH MINDSET

WEEK EIGHT

Focus of the Week:

You have completed the final week! Congratulations! Week Eight focused on maintaining your presence in your desired state by practicing internal and external anchoring techniques! I explained how internal anchoring involves all the mindset work you have done so far, while external anchoring requires managing your exposures and taking aligned actions.

I emphasized some mission-critical points about exposures: what you expose yourself to daily must highly align with what you want for yourself. This means being mindful about media consumption, social interactions, and other influences that could undermine your progress. I also introduced the concept of "Doing the Do's" - taking actions that support and reinforce your positive thought programs. I have a catalog of 33 additional anchoring techniques available to you in the appendix.

Finally, I explained the importance of mind-brain and body harmony and introduced two powerful techniques: Breathwork and the Emotional Freedom Technique (EFT). Remember—these are not bothersome homework assignments meant to keep you busy; they are essential tools to help you maintain your presence exactly where you want it to be!

Wrap-Up
Conclusion and Tips For Success

Conclusion

We have covered a lot in this book! Some things you may have heard before, and some things are probably new. Ultimately, you learned that harnessing the powers of your mind-brain is essential to obtaining a growth mindset. You learned that a growth mindset fosters positive experiences and enables you to be resilient, solve problems, and develop self-confidence. You further learned that a fixed mindset is very limiting and caused by aligning with and engaging in negative thought programs. You learned the difference between the mind and the brain and the ways in which they interact with each other. You learned that they are interconnected such that one supports and reinforces the other, creating a feedback loop that is always running in the subconscious mind. You learned that you have natural powers of neuroplasticity, which allow you to reprogram your thinking and generate new neural connections in your brain. But that is not all…

It seems to be a condition of being human that we tend to have a lot of negative content commanding our attention and running our mind-brains. We must understand that everyone experiences this and that it is 100% possible to change it. The mind is powerful and can override the brain's hardwiring, triggering neuroplasticity to develop new neural networks that reflect positive thought programs. Not even medication can do this. Medication is useful, sometimes even necessary, to control extreme symptoms. Still, medication cannot cause the establishment of new ways of thinking. You are the only one who truly has this power. If you are on medication, consider that it is a tool to assist you in this process, but it cannot do it for you. You must be an active doer!

As a rule, we want to limit the amount of time and energy we give to unwanted thoughts, feelings, and behaviors. This is a major difference between what I teach and many traditional therapeutic approaches. Sometimes, mostly with adults, we do need to spend time resolving problems developed by long-standing negative programs, but as a general rule, we always want to limit our interaction with the negative! Our attention and focus on negative content such as fear, anger, or sadness keep these negative programs online. Even if we are negating the negative, we are actually engaging with it, which only reinforces it. Kind of like trying to put a fire out with an accelerant like gas- it will only cause more fire.

Instead of paying attention to what makes us unhappy, we shift the focus of our attention onto what it is that we do want to experience. This involves clear intentions, focal points, and frequent shifting! It can feel awkward at first, and in the beginning, we often experience the ping-pong ball effect of bouncing back and forth from the negative to the positive. But do not worry; this phase only lasts a little while, and once you have developed your skills, you can anchor your presence where you want it. Why? Because you will have successfully developed new, positive thought programs and neural networks and, ultimately, a fresh place to "be from."

CONCLUSION AND TIPS FOR SUCCESS

Young people are really good at this and typically experience much more success than adults because their mind-brain's are developmentally more plastic. Also, unlike adults, they do not have to contend with years of established negatively programmed hardwiring.

"Doing the Do's" is mission critical! Without taking actions that are highly aligned with what you want for yourself, you can cancel all the hard, internal work you have already done. Mind your exposures, and do not self-sabotage! If you want to be happy and confident, you absolutely must reject gossip, doom scrolling on social media, comparing yourself to inauthentic people, and isolating yourself. Instead, appreciate yourself! Engage in learning pro-social behaviors (YouTube swapping topic!), seek out positively minded people, and focus your attention only on the thoughts and things that bring you joy. Anchoring yourself to this state will naturally draw in more of the same!

It is really important to add a "Do" that involves targeting the energetic connections between the mind, brain, and body or nervous system. This helps integrate all of your progress and remove or prevent "blocks" from thwarting your progress. By attending to your whole self, you will maximize your success.

Finally, imagine an awesome party happening atop a beautiful hillside. Everyone who is there are people you really love and want to be around. Maybe there are some potential new friends, too. It is purely a good time, and you are invited! Everyone wants you to come. But it is your job to show up. No one can do that for you. There are lots of ways to get there. But the hilltop will not flatten itself to the ground, nor will the party-goers relocate to bring the party to you. You have to get yourself there, which you are 100% capable of doing now that you know how. So, start walking, climbing, skipping, running, or whichever method you choose, and I promise you will be there before you know it!

14 Tips For Success

1. Visualize the process: Intention & Awareness-> Identification-> Rejection-> Separation-> Focal Points-> Shifting-> States & Aligned Experiences-> Anchoring

2. Now that you have completed the book and have been practicing the teachings along the way, commit to a time frame to go all in! Choose something reasonable, like two weeks. Fully apply what you have learned over the last eight weeks. After, reflect on how you feel and what those two weeks were like. Be authentic. Be real about it! Even if you only noticed small improvements, extend those improvements by devoting two more weeks. Why not? You have come this far. I guarantee you will see measurable progress in a month's time! Imagine how good you would feel if you kept on going!

3. Get prepared. That means having support- you do not need to do this alone. Do this with your parent(s), other family members/trusted adults, or even a therapist. What is the point in reading all of this if not?

4. Be consistent. If you take a step backward, move forward again without judging yourself. Self-judgment is the quickest way to self-sabotage and is a mind trap. No one is perfect, and everyone, including me, experiences interference from the negative. Remember the ping-pong ball effect when you first start shifting? It will decrease

with time and consistency. Just carry on.

5. Do all kinds of Do's. Try new things and expose yourself to new content and methods. One day, you will hear or see something you may have heard or seen before, but suddenly, it will click with you. Something about how it is presented will resonate with you and give you a whole new perspective!

6. Self-monitor and self-correct, self-monitor and self-correct, self-monitor and self-correct… Everyday!

7. Have clear, intentional focal points/destinations plugged into your internal GPS so that you are not haphazardly wandering around, hoping to land somewhere you think you might want to be. Be the captain of your own ship. The engine room is running and providing you with thrust. Direct it, steer it, lest you run your ship aground or find yourself hopelessly lost at sea.

8. Use natural points of the day to your benefit. Waking and bedtime are musts for all internal work!

9. Keep track of every success. The negative mind dismisses the positive and overly focuses on the negative to keep you ensnared. Own your successes no matter how small. If you write them down, you will be astounded at how many successes you actually experience.

10. Watch out for mind traps that distract and trick you, such as the "man behind the curtain," who would have you believe something different or worse than what is actually happening. Never accept mind traps; they are traps. Reject, separate, and shift away.

11. TALK! Communicate your thoughts and feelings. Even though this workbook is not about going to therapy, it

does not mean that you should not share how you are thinking and feeling with appropriate people like parents, trusted adults/other family members, or even a therapist. Talking provides us with support and helps us integrate what we are learning and experiencing so we can make the best use of it!

12. If you ever feel unsure of your thoughts, use Identification techniques: Congruency, the Interview with the Negative, or Running a Mind Diagnostic. But most of all, trust yourself! Always have faith in yourself and trust your intuition!

13. If you are struggling with a bout of strong negative thoughts, emotions, or behaviors that are difficult to control, flood yourself with positive anchoring techniques! Sometimes, we get overwhelmed and discouraged. I do, too. When this happens, I only read, watch, and listen (expose myself) to highly positive content that is in complete alignment with what I want for myself. If I am struggling with following my own internal mantras/affirmations, narratives, and visualizations, I will find guided meditations, breathing exercises, audiobooks, or high-frequency music to wake up or fall asleep to until I can switch my mind-brain back onto its right and proper track. Whatever you do, never allow a bout of negativity to go on unchecked. Do not accept these conditions for yourself! Use and apply your resources; that is why you have them!

14. Reread this workbook! We have covered many topics, and you have learned quite a bit. If you went back through it, I am certain you would pick up on even more things and may even have additional insights.

Now go forth and conquer!!

GROWTH MINDSET

References

Appelbaum, L. G., Shenasa, M. A., Stolz, L., & Daskalakis, Z. (2022). Synaptic plasticity and mental health: methods, challenges and opportunities. Neuropsychopharmacology, 48(1), 113–120. https://doi.org/10.1038/s41386-022-01370-w

Arnott, S. (2024, February 18). The backwards bicycle and neuroplasticity. The Emotional Intelligence Training Company. https://www.eitrainingcompany.com/2015/06/the-backwards-bicycle-and-neuroplasticity/

Dijkstra, N., & Fleming, S. M. (2021). Fundamental constraints on distinguishing reality from imagination [Preprint]. https://doi.org/10.31234/osf.io/bw872

Doidge, N. (2007). The brain that changes itself: Stories of personal triumph from the frontiers of brain science. Penguin Books.

Hanson, R. (2013). Hardwiring happiness: The new brain science of contentment, calm, and confidence. Harmony Books.

Heyes, S. B., Lau, J. Y. F., & Holmes, E. A. (2013). Mental imagery, emotion and psychopathology across child and adolescent development. Developmental Cognitive Neuroscience, 5, 119-134. https://doi.org/10.1016/j.dcn.2013.02.004

Heyes, S. B., Pictet, A., Mitchell, H., Raeder, S. M., Lau, J. Y. F., Holmes, E. A., & Blackwell, S. E. (2016). Mental imagery-based training to modify mood and cognitive bias in adolescents: Effects of valence and perspective. Cognitive Therapy and Research, 41(1), 73-85. https://doi.org/10.1007/s10608-016-9795-8

Hensch, T. K. (2015). Timing mechanisms of critical periods in brain development. Simons Foundation. https://www.simonsfoundation.org/event/timing-mechanisms-of-critical-periods-in-brain-development/

LifeXchange Solutions. (2019, September 1). Backwards brain bike right first-time: Cyclops challenge #1 [Video]. YouTube. https://www.youtube.com/watch?v=-Skv6ou64ek

Lipton, B. H. (2015). The biology of belief: Unleashing the power of consciousness, matter, and miracles (10th anniversary ed.). [Kindle version].

McAllister, K. (2023, January 23). Making and breaking connections in the brain. UC Davis Center for Neuroscience. https://neuroscience.ucdavis.edu/news/making-and-breaking-connections-brain

Robinson, J. (2024, May 10). A neuroscientist explains how your brain actually thinks. ScienceAlert. https://www.sciencealert.com/a-neuroscientist-explains-how-your-brain-actually-thinks

Simpkins, C. A., & Simpkins, A. M. (2012). Neuroplasticity and neurogenesis: Changing moment-by-moment. In Springer eBooks (pp. 165-174). https://doi.org/10.1007/978-1-4614-4842-6_13

Sweeton, J. (2017, November 15). Why you should do the corny, touchy-feely things recommended by your therapist. Psychology Today. https://www.psychologytoday.com/us/blog/workings-well-being/201711/change-your-brain-cognitive-therapy

Velikova, S., Sjaaheim, H., & Nordtug, B. (2017). Can the psycho-emotional state be optimized by regular use of positive imagery? Psychological and electroencephalographic study of self-guided training. Frontiers in Human Neuroscience, 10, Article 225407. https://doi.org/10.3389/fnhum.2016.00664

APPENDIX CONTENTS

Appendix: Catalog of Anchoring Techniques   **147**

**Part One: Internal Anchoring Techniques:
Apply Your Intentional Thinking Skills!**   **148**

Mantras/Affirmations

Narratives

Visualization/Mental Imagery

Mindfulness Exercises

Meditation

Progressive Relaxation

**Part Two: External Anchoring Techniques:
Mind your Exposures and Do the Do's!**   **151**

Breathwork

Energy Work   Emotional Freedom Technique (EFT)

Qi Gong/Tai Chi

Acupressure

Reiki

Nature

Do Outdoor Activities and Exercise in Nature

Earthing

Pursue Your Hobbies and Personal Interests

Learn and Do New Things

Use Technology

Mindfulness Phone Apps

Bio-Monitoring/Feedback Devices

Wearable Items

Biofeedback Devices

Protective Passive Body of Living Space Technologies

Energy Healing Frequency Technology

Organization Techniques

Vision Board

Large Visual Field Organizer

Adopt New Approaches to Your Routines

Reorganize Your Physical Space

Try Going to Therapy

Consider Learning Some Eye Movement Exercises

Health and Nutrition

Physical Movement

Vigorous Exercise

Somatic Exercise

Food

Water

Supplements

Sleep

Live to Your Fullest!

Part Three: Bonus Activity: The Rice Experiment   169

**Anchoring Techniques Conclusion:
   Be Intentional, Own Your Life   172**

Appendix

Catalog of Anchoring Techniques

In A Growth Mindset Workbook for Teens: A Practical 8-Week Guide to Cultivate Resilience, Solve Problems, and Ignite Confidence Using Clinically Crafted Activities for Real Life, you learned about the concept of "anchoring." Anchoring is the last phase of the Mind-Brain Connection approach and is mission-critical to achieving a lasting growth mindset. It involves employing specific techniques that contribute to anchoring you to your desired mental state. This is important because we know that established mental states tend to self-perpetuate by generating experiences consistent with the state. So- to avoid negative experiences, best ensure that you properly self-monitor, self-correct, and use effective anchoring techniques to obtain and maintain your chosen mental state!

Part One: Internal Anchoring Techniques

Apply Your Intentional Thinking Skills!

Internal anchoring is defined as all of the solid, internal work you have done so far—the thinking work, the mindfulness work, the visualization work, the understanding and learning work of how the mind affects the brain, how the brain creates physical structures known as neural networks to provide us with experiences consistent with our repetitive thoughts, and how neuroplasticity enables you to control your own experiences. You have done a lot of internal work!

Many of the techniques contained within the stages of Intention & Awareness, Identification, Rejection & Separation, Focal Points, Shifting, and States & Aligned Experiences focus on internal anchoring techniques. Of course, some are more action-based, but most are focused on internal mind-brain work. I will not re-write all of them here because you have the book! However, I will reiterate some very important ones and include a few pointers.

Mantras/Affirmations

Always evaluate and adjust these to suit your current life circumstances! You will come up with new ones as you progress. Listen to and read about other sources that teach mantras/affirmations because you may come across new ones that really speak to you. Try them out!

Narratives

Make sure these are in direct support of and align with your mantras/affirmations, or, what it is you truly want for yourself! Most people find it easy to connect to a real-life situation when working with narratives, but you can come up with anything you want!

Visualization/Mental Imagery

This technique is used and taught by literally every person teaching self-improvement- no matter the industry or profession (business, sports, health, psychology, or spirituality). We must visualize what we truly want for ourselves and connect to it emotionally. Vivid visualization from the experiencer's perspective (first person) activates the regions of the brain associated with your imagery. The brain does not care that you are not physically having the experience! This makes visualization a powerful technique to activate neuroplasticity- because you can literally shape new neural connections with the power of your mind! This practice should always be used as often as possible, but definitely upon waking and before going to sleep. Never start or end your day by running negative thought programs, being in a negative state, or visualizing negative things. This is mission-critical!

Mindfulness Exercises

Consider learning some basic mindfulness techniques. I think I can safely say that 100% of all people could benefit from increasing their ability to be mindful. I must admit, I am usually leery of making such definitive statements as "100% of all people," but I am sticking to my guns on this one. Heck, since I am at it, I will double down and throw in a couple more "100 %ers": 100% of all people could benefit from increasing their ability to be mindful, loving, compassionate, gracious, and thankful. The practice of mindfulness exercises can increase all of these!

Meditation

Most people cringe when I suggest trying meditation because it can be difficult! Remember in the book when I referenced the Buddhist Monks in Week Two about Intention and Awareness and how they devote themselves to mindfulness practices like meditation? They clearly have highly developed abilities, but you do not need "monk-level" skills to benefit. The general rule is that you are simply practicing being still in the mind and often also in the body, although there are such things as movement meditations, like walking meditations, if you want to pursue the variations. The point of quieting the mind is to shut down the noisy influence of the negative and calm down the stress reactions of the body. Doing so will bring about a greater sense of peace and well-being while allowing you to better connect with positive energies like your intuition, spirit, or God. There is literally no downside to this!

Progressive Relaxation

This is a type of meditation in which you use your mind to scan how your body feels, focus on points of tension, and then release that tension. Following an expert's guided progressive relaxation exercise is often helpful in learning the process and knowing where to focus. It typically involves tightening up specific areas of your body, visualizing certain colors or energies, and then releasing that tension. There are many variations. Progressive relaxation is helpful when you feel like your body just will not relax or is pent-up with stressful energy.

Part Two: External Anchoring Techniques

Mind Your Exposures and Do the Do's!

If you recall in the book, external anchoring is the last yet very impactful process required to create new, positive, and lasting experiences for yourself. It involves reducing "exposures" to negative influences and adding actions to support your internal work. "Doing to Do's" propels your progress forward, causing a catalyst effect with respect to neuroplasticity. This is because you are pairing action-based measures with your intentional thinking skills, essentially solidifying new "hardwiring" through multiple sources and types of reinforcement. Most people unwittingly do this all day, every day, except with negative thinking and corresponding negative behaviors! The book taught us how this traps us into negative states!

Breathwork

I included breathwork in the book because when used as part of your normal routine, it is highly effective at bringing about positive change. Breathwork can calm the nervous system almost immediately (shutting down the sympathetic nervous system and activating the parasympathetic), help detox the body, oxygenate the blood, quiet the mind, and help realign our energy systems throughout the body. In more intense practices, it is also known to release a natural hormone known as DMT, which allows us to feel peaceful and connected to others and things around us.

Many people feel that breathwork benefits the spirit and helps us connect to higher levels of consciousness. There really is no downside- especially with so many variations from which to choose, such as breath counting, box breathing, breath "scraping," and perhaps the most odd-looking one- full, active breathing that can also be fast. If you look up breathwork on the internet, you will see all kinds of people performing and teaching it, from yoga practitioners to reiki masters to health gurus and athletes of all types. There is a breathwork practitioner and technique for everyone and every situation!

Energy Work

Energy is everything. It is everywhere. It is what we are, what our thoughts are, and what our world is made up of. It is universal. It is the universe. It cannot be created or destroyed. Do I sound like your science teacher yet? Since everything known is made of energy, it is probably not a bad idea to learn about some techniques that focus on increasing positive energies!

Emotional Freedom Technique (EFT)

I also included this technique in the book because it is evidence-based, effective, and easy! You simply tap on specific points of the head, torso, and side of your hand while using your mantras/affirmations. The points are meridian points that, when tapped on, help realign your energies, calm the mind and body, and program in your new, positive intentions and neural networks. It is also known as "tapping in" your mantras/affirmations. All you need to do is watch a quick video to see what it looks like, or you can download an image from the internet that shows you the points to tap on. This technique is so simple but very powerful. Since you are working on positive self-think/talk anyway, you may as well tap a little simultaneously!

Qi Gong/Tai Chi

These are specific exercises performed with slow and controlled motions designed to correct, open, and align energy in the body and mind. Breathing is also involved. Qi gong can also be done seated or completely still. These two disciplines are peaceful but powerful, and they also boost mindfulness! They are similar and often referred to as "internal martial arts."

Acupressure

Acupressure is a Traditional Chinese Medicine (TCM) technique of applying pressure to specific points on the body that follow meridian energy lines. Depending on where the points are located, pressing on them can be helpful for different problems. Maps of these locations on the body can easily be found on the internet. Some companies even make socks that have maps on the bottom of the feet, so you know where to press for what problem!

Reiki

Reiki is a Japanese technique that uses a practitioner's hands to direct and channel "universal life force" energy in the body. It improves energy flow and assists in removing stuck or blocked energy. Although Reiki is typically done with light hand touching, healing can also be delivered at a distance by "sending" the energy.

Nature

Go be in it! Observe it! Be one with it! Nature is your friend, friend.

Do Outdoor Activities and Exercise in Nature

Sit, pose, meditate, walk, run, hike, bike, paddle, climb, ride...you get the point. Just go outside—preferably with fresh air and flora and fauna!

Earthing

I referenced this in the book in the section about shifting. Earthing is the practice of connecting and synchronizing yourself to the energies of the earth. It is also sometimes referred to as grounding to the Earth. You can do this in water as well. Essentially, you can drain off accumulated negative, stuck energies that are not good for your physical or mental health and take on free electrons that are good for you from the Earth or water. "Earthers" often describe the Earth as a giant battery that, when we connect to it, helps recharge us.

There are many products nowadays that assist with grounding ourselves to the Earth's energy. Some examples are all-natural fiber clothing, shoes, bedding, and pulsed electromagnetic field therapy (PEMF) technologies like mats or mattress pads that assist with grounding when we cannot be outside in direct connection with the Earth. It is really cool to see someone holding a voltage meter while grounded versus ungrounded. When grounded, the meter shows a drop in voltage almost instantaneously!

Pursue Your Hobbies and Personal Interests

This is very important! By doing so, you are cultivating creative energy, which is a powerful force because it enhances our ability to create or generate things! It does not matter the topic or subject. What are we ultimately looking to do for ourselves? That is right, create positive experiences! So, engaging in anything creative only enhances your ability to create or generate whatever it is that you want for yourself.

Learn and Do New Things

Engaging in new learning and trying new things is essential for growth. Do not worry because I am not suggesting that you undertake large endeavors like learning a new language or reading a volume of books (although I would never discourage this)! However, any type of learning stimulates your brain by creating new neural networks, opens your mind to different experiences, helps with mental flexibility, and provides fresh perspectives. Learning new things can only enrich you!

Use Technology

You might think that I would be against using technology, given everything I said in the book about the negative effects of media, social media, and gaming. However, there is actually some great tech out there that assists us with attaining positive states!

Mindfulness Phone Apps

There are a lot of these! They can provide you with many types of guided meditations/visualizations, relaxation techniques, bedtime stories, soothing music, and even the ability to track your progress. If staying off your phone at bedtime seems impossible, ensure you only use it to engage with "Jill-approved" stuff! You have a pass for using your phone to access an app teaching you life-enriching techniques like going to sleep with a positive mindset! I know, I know... this is kind of like being told you can eat as much as you like, as long as it is green and leafy. Boo, Jill, boo!

Bio-Monitoring/Feedback Devices

These devices monitor different functional aspects of your physical body.

Wearable Items

Watches or rings can provide daily feedback about your sleep, temperature, heart rate, and activity levels. They are useful for collecting data and displaying measurements and graphs representing increases or decreases in your body's response to whatever techniques you are implementing. Psychologically speaking, it is reinforcing to see positive changes happening! It encourages us to keep going! On the downside, sometimes people get too fixated on the data and panic when it is not moving in the right direction. This is counterproductive and can undermine progress by inadvertently creating a source of stress. As such, while useful, I recommend these devices be used mindfully to look at "the big picture" over a predetermined span of time and not on short-term data points.

Biofeedback Devices

Some tech specifically measures things like heart rate variability (HRV) or brainwave patterns (quantitative electroencephalography or qEEG). HRV and brainwaves are biological functions that we aim to measure and manipulate in the short term while using the device. By doing so, we can train ourselves to control these biological functions long-term, which is very useful! Imagine having greater control over the feedback loop between the mind-brain and the body!

The technology prompts you how to change or regulate your biological activity. It is really cool and no longer looks like a crazy science experiment where someone is wearing a colander on their head with wires coming out while staring at a screen! Some companies specialize in wearable devices like headbands for monitoring brainwaves; others have finger/earlobe clips or handheld devices for measuring HRV. Volumes of research exist on the benefits of both HRV and qEEG biofeedback, and the results are pretty amazing.

Protective Passive Body or Living Space Technologies

This type of tech is a must because our environment is flooded with electromagnetic frequencies (EMFs) 24/7/365. Whether we like it or not, our modern-day society revolves around the technology of the internet, cell phones, cell towers, wi-fi routers, televisions, computers, Bluetooth devices, and other "smart" things. All of those EMFs floating around create something called electromagnetic smog, and it negatively impacts our mental and physical health. The good news is that you do not need to resort to wearing a tinfoil hat! Nowadays, many types of protective devices exist that are useful in reducing or blocking out this smog! Some are just objects, like certain crystals, stones, wearable metals, and holographic discs/stickers. In contrast, others are technologies in and of themselves that plug into your computer or wall outlet to counteract and dissipate EMFs. Some can even emit healthier energies!

Energy Healing Frequency Technology

I love frequency technology because there are many different types to choose from and also because you do not have to do anything- you typically just sit there! Some examples are rife frequencies, light frequencies (phototherapy), sound frequencies, PEMF (see Earthing), and scalar waves (EESystem). This category could easily be an entire book all by itself– which perhaps I will create for you in the near future because the topic is just so cool!

In the meantime, if you want to try it out for free, just look up "sound frequency healing" on the internet. You will discover music and tones that have been specifically tuned to frequencies associated with the health of the human mind, body, and energy field.

Brainwave entrainment is an example of sound frequency healing. Specific frequencies are played either ambiently (isochronic tones) or sometimes require headphones (binaural beats) because different frequencies are played into each ear. The purpose is to regulate brainwave activity or alter it to achieve a purpose, such as sleep or concentration. I use sound frequencies all of the time, including right now, while writing this ebook! In fact, I rarely undertake a strenuous mental activity like writing for hours without using supportive frequencies simultaneously!

Organization Techniques

The art of organization goes beyond simple tidying - it is about creating systems that help your mind and environment work harmoniously. Whether you want to streamline your thoughts for better productivity or transform your physical space into a more functional setting, effective organization techniques can make a profound difference in your daily life. By implementing thoughtful strategies for both mental and physical organization, you can reduce stress, increase efficiency, and create an environment that supports your goals.

Vision Board

This is a simple but powerful technique for keeping what it is you that you want for yourself at the forefront of your mind every day. The anchoring technique of internal visualization is still necessary; however, using a vision board also provides an external visualization source. It assists with consistency and reinforcing yourself, and is also fun to make! You get to design it any way that suits you by posting images that are highly aligned with what it is you want for yourself. Get creative and make it large! Gaze at it daily and imagine experiencing what you see.

Large Visual Field Organizer

Anyone who has trouble with lists or agenda planners should try this!

Find a large blank spot on a wall or perhaps the backside of a door or closet door. You can use poster-sized sticky notes or painter's tape. You will also need various small, colored sticky notes. This area will become a large visual field, as opposed to a small one like a list or calendar on your phone.

Changing the chart size from small to large is purposeful. The brain processes information differently when looking at a small, centralized visual field versus a large, peripheral one. First, the information is always in your line of sight and color-coded, making recall much easier. Second, the larger the field, the more expansive our information processing is. We tend to literally see "the bigger picture," which helps us avoid fixating on small details or getting "tunnel vision." In fact, when I write, I prefer to use a large, TV-sized screen farther away from my face than my laptop screen. It is actually 4-5 feet away and on another table. Sometimes, I will sit back even further and just look at the words and the layout. It is a strategy that I use to ensure an overall flow to my writing so I do not get bogged down in details!

Okay, so now you will create a very large chart with five columns for the days of the week and two rows for morning (am) and afternoon (pm). Next, divide your responsibilities for the week into categories such as chores, school, work, appointments, etc. Each category needs to be represented with a different-colored sticky note. Write your weekly obligations and responsibilities on the sticky notes, making sure they match the color of the chosen categories.

Now, stick them up on the chart where they belong, either in the morning or afternoon of each day. You do not need to add hours to the chart, but you can write the times on each sticky note (if a specific time is required) and then place them in order. So, if you have something to do at 1:00 pm, make sure that sticky note is above the ones that need to happen later in the day or have no specific time requirement. Stand back and look at the chart. You should see various colors throughout the week, representing the different categories of your responsibilities.

Your goal is to achieve balance on your chart. Does one day have a lot of empty space? Is another day piled up with sticky notes? Are there all one color of sticky notes in one place but not in others? Begin moving around the notes that can go to different days and times to achieve balance and flow.

Now all you need to do is take a glancing walk past the chart to know what you must do for the week because the amount of sticky notes per day will tell you how many responsibilities you have, and the colors will indicate in which category. You may not even need to walk up and read the sticky notes to realize what you have to do.

As you complete your tasks, removing them from the wall is important. It helps declutter the brain, provides a sense of accomplishment, and is also necessary for your week-in-review analysis. However, keep the notes because we are creatures of habit and you will likely need many of the same ones again the following week.

Finally, analyze your week. Are there still notes on the wall at the end of the week? If so, why? Is there something that you could have done differently, or was it due to situations outside of your control? Did you overbook yourself or not use time wisely? Did you accomplish more than you thought you did? Oftentimes, it just seems like we have piles of unmanageable responsibilities when, in reality, it is not the case. The mind-brain tends to overly focus on this perception, producing a sense of overwhelm, dread, and defeat that causes us to procrastinate or mentally shut down. But when we can cognitively re-arrange and physically manipulate our tasks, we can override this tendency and literally see that we can be much more productive most of the time!

As a side note, the large visual field organization chart is also useful for other purposes, like keeping track of groups of people's responsibilities. For families, it can be modified so everyone has their own colored sticky notes. This way, everyone can easily see who has which responsibilities, tasks, or even appointments. Play around with this technique to see how it works best for you.

Adopt New Approaches to Your Routines

In the workbook, one of the exercises in the anchoring section was to gather data on how you spent your day from the time of waking up to going to bed. Do you rush? Do you spend excessive time on less important activities than necessary ones? Could you substitute a new interest or hobby for one that does not serve you or align with your goals? How can you fit more positive routines into your day?

For example, did you realize you could do your internal anchoring exercises before you even got out of bed in the morning? There is no reason to look for extra time in the day. Instead of watching mindless or negative content on the internet, substitute only positive content with which you are highly aligned! These are simple swap-outs that do not require finding extra time or making huge changes but have a big payoff!

Reorganize Your Physical Space

Cluttered spaces reflect cluttered minds! Clutter and mess

prevent the natural flow of energy and can lead to imbalances and blocked energy. Try a minimalist approach. How much stuff do you actually use, wear, or need? Try to eliminate everything you do not use regularly and either donate or pack it up and store it in a different location. Avoid bins! They tend to turn into garbage cans. Better to remove as much as possible from your personal space and get down to the bare necessities. You will find that you feel much better in a clean, organized, and clear space.

Try Going to Therapy

There is no downside to this, sayeth the clinical therapist! Talking is good because it helps solve problems, allows you to reflect on your progress with a neutral person, and assists you in implementing everything you are learning. You do not need to go forever, but everyone needs support when doing self-work! You want to set yourself up for success, not failure! Even if you start working with a therapist and it does not feel like a good fit, that is ok! It is no big deal. With the advent and prevalence of telehealth, you can find someone else pretty quickly.

Consider Learning Some Eye Movement Exercises

Eye movement exercises assist with releasing negative emotions and the effects of negative memories stored within the brain. There are different types of eye movement approaches. Some are very structured, such as Eye Movement Desensitization and Reprocessing (EMDR) and Brainspotting therapy, which require pairing tapping-like exercises and sometimes binaural sound while working with a trained therapist. However, there are also some basic eye movement exercises that you can do on your own, which you can even pair with the EFT tapping you have already learned about.

Scientists do not completely understand why using specific eye movements coupled with bilateral stimulation (tapping on both sides of the body or listening to different frequencies in each ear) can help alleviate anxiety and stress from painful memories other than acknowledging it seems to unlock or unblock negative neural networks. Regardless, the research has shown that it works. If this interests you, look up some basic self-guided eye movement meditations to try it out!

Health and Nutrition

Maintaining physical health with exercise, nutrition, water, and sleep is paramount to achieving a healthy mind-brain. If our body is stressed, in poor health, and loaded with toxins, it is very difficult even to think straight!

Physical Movement

Engaging in both vigorous and somatic exercises is very good for you! The more you practice mindfulness, the better you become at interpreting whether your body needs intense exercise or more soothing, relaxing movements. Sometimes, you will find yourself engaging in one or the other for periods of time before intuitively knowing that you need to switch. Just know that our minds and bodies need a balance of both for optimal health.

Vigorous Exercise

This category includes team sports or individual activities such as running/walking, swimming, biking, tennis, golf, canoe/kayak, hiking, weight lifting, martial arts, etc. Not only is exercise good for our physical body, but when we move the body, we also move the mind! Oftentimes, when people find themselves mentally stuck, moving your body will enable your mind to move as well. So, if you have writer's block, are experiencing looping repetitive thinking, or just feel mentally unproductive- Move!

Somatic Exercise

Somatic exercises are typically slow, soothing, mindful movements that assist with managing stiffness/pain, increasing the mind-brain and body connection, and balancing our energy field. The focus is on the internal experience as opposed to an external goal of lifting more weight or running farther. I described Qi Gong and Tai Chi above under the category of Energy Work, but they also apply to this category. Yoga can be more active and involves deep stretching, strengthening poses, and breathwork.

Food

I do not need to say a lot here because I am certain you know the rules: Your body needs vegetables, whole foods, and good protein sources to function properly. This is another very important topic dense with information that cannot be adequately covered in a few paragraphs!

Just know that processed and fried foods lack nutritional value and have additives that are not good for our bodies. Some of those additives are actually toxic, so much so that other countries have made putting them in their food either at all or at the same levels that we do in the U.S., illegal! Naming them all will cause a serious digression, so I will just drop that fact on you, which you can research further if interested. Go ahead- fact-check me! I welcome it because I know how much you would learn in the process :)

Although sugar is found everywhere, it is terrible for us. It tastes good but is addictive, so we crave it. The more sugar you eat, the more you crave it. Sugar, fried, and processed foods put our bodies into an acidic state, which is terrible for our immune system. These types of foods also wreak havoc across all other bodily functions, from metabolism to cognitive functioning. Please try to be good to your body by adding whole, fresh foods, leafy greens, and other vegetables to your diet whenever possible! Try growing a vegetable or two, even if you only have a windowsill!

Water

Drink a lot of it, but make sure it is as free from contaminants as possible. Water sourced from city water is always treated with chemicals like chlorine and fluoride to benefit our health and prevent contamination from pesticides, microorganisms, and pharmaceutical products, but these chemicals are not necessarily good for us. Furthermore, the chemical additives can break down into other, more harmful compounds, creating secondary contaminants.

Recent studies have determined that fluoride lowers children's intelligence at levels present in some of our city-sourced drinking water. As with food additives, many other countries have made it illegal to fluoridate their drinking water or to fluoridate it at the levels found in our water. One must wonder why this could be.

Groundwater can also contain contaminants, depending on where you live and where your well is located. Test kits can help you determine the quality of your well water. Regardless, filtering your water before you drink is always a good idea.

There are many options for water filtering methods and products—it is an entire industry! I am a big fan of alkalizing and structuring my water. Eating and drinking "alkaline" is an approach to health meant to support our immune systems and decrease the amount of acid and toxic loads in our bodies.

Structuring water is when you take regular, lifeless tap water, filter it for contaminants, and move it through a special type of vortex, like a magnetized funnel, to change the shape and energy of the water molecules. Nature actually does this herself when water runs through unpolluted streams, rivers, and springs. It passes over sand, rocks, and different types of crystals and minerals, adding energy to the water and changing the shape of the molecules, making them more hydrating and beneficial to our bodies. Many scientists even consider that once water is structured, it becomes a fourth phase of water, a crystalline phase!

This is an exciting area of research! Structuring water has so many positive health implications, and it is fun and easy to do. You can even create your own process! If you research this topic a bit, you will see people who have created inspiring structuring systems that look like works of art.

Supplements

Our bodies need proper amounts of nutrients in the form of vitamins and minerals to function properly. Most of our food either does not have enough nutrients or has been "enriched" with low-quality nutrients. It is best to find good quality supplements to take regularly to address this issue.

Additionally, you can look to supplement yourself with something called nootropics. Nootropics are combinations of specific vitamins, minerals, and nutrients meant to increase brain health and cognitive functioning. Some are designed to improve memory, attention/focus, cognitive endurance, mood, and even sleep. This is a booming, emerging market, so you do not need to dig deep to find nootropics, although you do need to be cautious about choosing the right product. Also, I should note that with any supplement, expect to go through some trial and error before finding something that works best for you. Unfortunately, this can get pricey if you have not done good foundational research.

Sleep

Get eight or more hours of good, quality sleep! Your body and brain depend on sleep to heal, regenerate, and grow. Less than eight hours is inadequate for most people, especially children and teenagers. Sorry, there are no workarounds for proper sleep quantity and quality, but there are ways to improve it.

I think you know what I am about to say next, but I have to say it anyway, so you might want to brace yourself! No food (especially junk food), drinks other than clean water, bad moods, phones, screens, social media, or LED lights immediately before or while in bed. Gaming is out of the question! Commonly accepted time frames for ending gaming before bedtime is about four hours! That is how long it takes for your brain to settle down after you have hyper-stimulated it with video games.

The good news about the "no phones" rules is the pass I gave you earlier in the Mindfulness Phone Apps section. If you recall, I stated that the exception is if you are using your phone to play high-frequency, calming music or listen to guided meditations.

Finally, learn about good sleep hygiene, which refers to practicing good sleep behaviors and providing yourself with a good sleeping environment. Replace bad sleep behaviors with good ones so that you develop healthier routines. Replacing behaviors is always easier than quitting bad ones, so set yourself up for success by swapping out bad choices for better ones. Do not forget to look forward to bed because you get to spend time on your positive visualizations while you fall asleep. Maximize this natural point of access to your subconscious mind and program it with all good things!

Live to Your Fullest!

Play! Have fun! Create! Be Curious! Never Stop Learning and Exploring!

Part Three: Bonus Activity

The Rice Experiment

Dr. Masaru Emoto (1943-2014) was a Japanese researcher who was famous for performing experiments on water. He wrote several books, one of which was a 2004 New York Times bestseller called The Hidden Messages in Water. He also made a film in 2004 called Messages from Water. His work was featured in other documentaries such as the 2004 What the Bleep Do We Know and the 2005 superhero movie Kamen Rider: The First. His work is considered controversial in mainstream channels, and a quick internet search yields Wikipedia results that seem strongly unfavorable.

His books, movies, and experiments are famous for demonstrating that our thoughts and intentions can affect water molecules and their physical structure. He performed experiments where he labeled water containers with positive and negative words/phrases and then also spoke those words to the water. He then froze the water. Later, he observed the ice crystals of the frozen water under a microscope and reportedly discovered some amazing results!

He found that the crystals from different containers had differing shapes, and some were even discolored. He reported that the crystals from the water that were spoken to positively had beautiful, symmetrical, snowflake-like shapes. In contrast, the crystals from the water that were spoken to negatively had asymmetrical shapes, some of which even looked like brown blobs.

He repeated these experiments in different ways, such as using sound. Also, he began branching out to look at water crystals from sources such as mountain streams, tap water, or polluted water. His results were consistent with his original findings. He concluded that water was programmable through thoughts, intentions, and environmental conditions and that drinking the water could have implications for our health. He also suggested that since our bodies are predominantly made of water, our health could be impacted by the nature of our thoughts, intentions, and environmental conditions.

Dr. Emoto even experimented with rice. He placed rice and water in three jars. He labeled two of the jars, one with the words "Thank you" and one with the words "You're an idiot." He did not label the third jar. For 30 days, he spoke the labeled words in a heartfelt manner to each jar. He ignored the third jar. By the end of the 30 days, he found that the "thank you" jar had fermented rice that possessed a pleasant smell. He found that the "you're an idiot" jar had moldy, black rice, but the ignored jar was the worst affected and rotting!

He concluded that words and intentions were indeed powerful things, strong enough to prevent decay or cause rotting. He further suggested that these results should be considered when raising children and that those exposed to neglectful conditions could be far more negatively affected than previously thought.

This experiment has been reproduced many times. A search on YouTube will pull up many people's results that seem consistent with Dr. Emoto's results. I even did this experiment–twice! When I did it, I used many jars with different words/phrases, and I even put different types of crystals on top of some of the jars. My results were also consistent with Dr. Emoto's results!

However, internet searches always seem to pull up very unfavorable and critical expert opinions about Dr. Emoto and his methodologies. This seems curious to me, as so many people have reproduced these experiments over the years. Are all his best-selling book buyers and "non-experts" making it up?

The only way to find out is to do this experiment for yourself!

It is fun and very easy to do. I recommend getting creative and adding more jars besides the original three. You can also consider using different types of water (tap, filtered, structured) and maybe even some stones or crystals (but you will need three versions of each).

Some other recommendations based on my experience are to use tightly sealable glass jars you do not plan to reuse! Even if you sterilize the jars with bleach and hot water, the "yuk" factor was a little too high for me to want to reuse them. I wanted to control for as many factors as possible in my homemade experiment, so I bought and used mason jars from the same source. I rinsed them and made sure they were completely dry. Then, I added rice and enough water to cover the rice from the same source. I also separated the jars into groups of three in different rooms to try and prevent them from getting positive or negative "vibe" crossover by being too clustered together.

Regardless of whether or not you choose to dive into this experiment, the results of Dr. Emoto's research demonstrate profound implications regarding the effect our thoughts, intentions, and environmental conditions have on our water. Furthermore, since our bodies are primarily comprised of water... WHOA!

Finally, I encourage you to watch his documentary or read his books for yourself. No matter what, you should also look at the images of the water crystals- they are simply amazing. I used to keep some posted in my office as a reminder of the power of thought and intention!

Anchoring Techniques Conclusion

Be Intentional, Own Your Life

The anchoring techniques outlined in this section represent a comprehensive toolbox for maintaining and strengthening your mind-brain, leading to an overall growth mindset. From internal practices like visualization and meditation to external supports like technology and environmental organization, each method serves as a powerful anchor for your desired mental state. Remember that you do not need to implement every technique at once – start with what resonates most strongly with you and gradually expand your practice.

The science is clear: our thoughts, intentions, and environment profoundly impact our neural pathways and, consequently, our experiences. By consistently applying these anchoring techniques, you are not just temporarily shifting your mindset – you are literally rewiring your brain for more positive, growth-oriented patterns of thinking and being.

Whether you practice mindfulness, reorganize your space, or conduct your own rice experiment, each step strengthens your foundation for lasting positive change. Your journey toward personal growth is unique, and these tools are here to support you along the way. Trust in the process, stay committed to your practice, and watch as your intentional efforts create meaningful transformation in your life!

APPENDIX